Think on These Things

J. Krishnamurti

Think on These Things

edited by D. Rajagopal

PERENNIAL LIBRARY
Harper & Row, Publishers
New York and Evanston

This book is published in Great Britain under the title: *This Matter of Culture.*

First PERENNIAL LIBRARY edition published 1970

9-74

Contents

Editor's Note

Whether writing about a conversation with someone, or describing a sunset, or giving a public talk, Krishnamurti seems to have a way of addressing his remarks, not just to his immediate audience, but to anyone, anywhere, who will listen; and there are many, all over the world, who are eager to listen. For, what he says is without bias, and universal, and in a strangely moving way reveals the very roots of our human problems.

The material contained in this volume was originally presented in the form of talks to students, teachers and parents in India, but its keen penetration and lucid simplicity will be deeply meaningful to thoughtful people everywhere, of all ages, and in every walk of life. Krishnamurti examines with characteristic objectivity and insight the expressions of what we are pleased to call our culture, our education, religion, politics and tradition; and he throws much light on such basic motivations as ambition, greed and envy, the desire for security and the lust for power—all of which he shows to be deteriorating factors in human society. According to Krishnamurti, real culture is neither a matter of breeding, nor of learning, nor of talent, nor even of genius, but it is what he calls "the timeless movement to find happiness, God, truth." And "when this movement is blocked by authority, by tradition, by fear, there is decay," regardless of the gifts or the accomplishments of any particular individual, race or civilization. He points out with uncompromising directness the false elements in our attitudes and institutions, and the implications of his remarks are profound and far-reaching.

A few words occur here and there in the text—*guru*, *sannyasi*, *puja* and *mantram*—with which western readers may not be entirely familiar, and they are therefore briefly explained here. A *guru* is a spiritual teacher; a *sannyasi* is a monk who has taken the final vows of renunciation according to Hindu rites; *puja* is the Hindu ritual worship; and a *mantram* is a sacred verse, hymn, or chant.

I

The Function of Education

I wonder if we have ever asked ourselves what education means. Why do we go to school, why do we learn various subjects, why do we pass examinations and compete with each other for better grades? What does this so-called education mean, and what is it all about? This is really a very important question, not only for the students, but also for the parents, for the teachers, and for everyone who loves this earth. Why do we go through the struggle to be educated? Is it merely in order to pass some examinations and get a job? Or is it the function of education to prepare us while we are young to understand the whole process of life? Having a job and earning one's livelihood is necessary—but is that all? Are we being educated only for that? Surely, life is not merely a job, an occupation; life is something extraordinarily wide and profound, it is a great mystery, a vast realm in which we function as human beings. If we merely prepare ourselves to earn a livelihood, we shall miss the whole point of life; and to understand life is much more important than merely to prepare for examinations and become very proficient in mathematics, physics, or what you will.

So, whether we are teachers or students, is it not important to ask ourselves why we are educating or being educated? And what does life mean? Is not life an extraordinary thing? The birds, the flowers, the flourishing trees, the heavens, the stars, the rivers and the fish therein—all this is life. Life is the poor and the rich; life is the constant battle between groups, races and nations; life is meditation; life is what we call religion, and it is also the subtle, hidden things of the mind—the envies, the ambitions, the passions, the fears, fulfilments and anxieties. All this and much more is life. But we generally prepare ourselves to understand only one small corner of it. We pass certain examinations, find a job, get married, have children, and then become more and more like machines. We remain fearful, anxious, frightened of life. So, is it the function of education to help us understand the whole process of life, or is it merely to prepare us for a vocation, for the best job we can get?

What is going to happen to all of us when we grow to be men and women? Have you ever asked yourselves what you are going to do when you grow up? In all likelihood you will get married, and before you know where you are you will be mothers and fathers; and you will then be tied to a job, or to the kitchen, in which you will gradually wither away. Is that all that *your* life is going to be? Have you ever asked yourselves this question? Should you not ask it? If your family is wealthy you may have a fairly good position already assured, your father may give you a comfortable job, or you may get richly married; but there also you will decay, deteriorate. Do you see?

Surely, education has no meaning unless it helps you to understand the vast expanse of life with all its subtleties, with its extraordinary beauty, its sorrows and joys. You may earn degrees, you may have a series of letters after your name and land a very good job; but then what? What is the point of it all if in the process your mind becomes dull, weary, stupid? So, while you are young, must you not seek to find out what life is all about? And is it not the true function of education to cultivate in you the intelligence which will try to find the answer to all these problems? Do you know what intelligence is? It is the capacity, surely, to think freely, without fear, without a formula, so that you begin to discover for yourself what is real, what is true; but if you are frightened you will never be intelligent. Any form of ambition, spiritual or mundane, breeds anxiety, fear; therefore ambition does not help to bring about a mind that is clear, simple, direct, and hence intelligent.

You know, it is really very important while you are young to live in an environment in which there is no fear. Most of us, as we grow older, become frightened; we are afraid of living, afraid of losing a job, afraid of tradition, afraid of what the neighbours, or what the wife or husband would say, afraid of death. Most of us have fear in one form or another; and where there is fear there is no intelligence. And is it not possible for all of us, while we are young, to be in an environment where there is no fear but rather an atmosphere of freedom—freedom, not just to do what we like, but to understand the whole process of living? Life is really very beautiful, it is not this ugly thing that we have made of it; and you can appreciate its richness, its depth, its extraordinary loveliness only when you revolt against everything—against organized religion, against tradition, against the present rotten society—so that you as a human being find out for yourself what is true. Not to imitate but to discover—*that* is education, is it not? It is very easy to conform to what your society or your parents and teachers tell you. That is a safe and easy way of existing; but that is not living, because in it there is fear, decay, death. To live is to find out for yourself what is true, and you can do this only when there is freedom, when there is continuous revolution inwardly, within yourself.

But you are not encouraged to do this; no one tells

you to question, to find out for yourself what God is, because if you were to rebel you would become a danger to all that is false. Your parents and society want you to live safely, and you also want to live safely. Living safely generally means living in imitation and therefore in fear. Surely, the function of education is to help each one of us to live freely and without fear, is it not? And to create an atmosphere in which there is no fear requires a great deal of thinking on your part as well as on the part of the teacher, the educator.

Do you know what this means—what an extraordinary thing it would be to create an atmosphere in which there is no fear? And we *must* create it, because we see that the world is caught up in endless wars; it is guided by politicians who are always seeking power; it is a world of lawyers, policemen and soldiers, of ambitious men and women all wanting position and all fighting each other to get it. Then there are the so-called saints, the religious *gurus* with their followers; they also want power, position, here or in the next life. It is a mad world, completely confused, in which the communist is fighting the capitalist, the socialist is resisting both, and everybody is against somebody, struggling to arrive at a safe place, a position of power or comfort. The world is torn by conflicting beliefs, by caste and class distinctions, by separative nationalities, by every form of stupidity and cruelty—and this is the world you are being educated to fit into. You are encouraged to fit into the framework of this disastrous society; your parents want you to do that, and you also want to fit in.

Now, is it the function of education merely to help you to conform to the pattern of this rotten social order, or is it to give you freedom—complete freedom to grow and create a different society, a new world? We want to have this freedom, not in the future, but now, otherwise we may all be destroyed. We must create immediately an atmosphere of freedom so that you can live and find out for yourselves what is true, so that you become intelligent, so that you are able to face the world and understand it, not just conform to it, so that inwardly, deeply, psychologically you are in constant revolt; because it is only those who are in constant revolt that discover what is true, not the man who conforms, who follows some tradition. It is only when you are constantly inquiring, constantly observing, constantly learning, that you find truth, God, or love; and you cannot inquire, observe, learn, you cannot be deeply aware, if you are afraid. So the function of education, surely, is to eradicate, inwardly as well as outwardly, this fear that destroys human thought, human relationship and love.

Questioner: If all individuals were in revolt, don't you think there would be chaos in the world?

KRISHNAMURTI: Listen to the question first, because it is very important to understand the question and not just wait for an answer. The question is: if all individuals were in revolt, would not the world be in chaos? But is the present society in such perfect order that chaos would result if everyone revolted against it? Is there not chaos *now?* Is everything beautiful, uncorrupted? Is everyone living happily, fully, richly? Is man not against man? Is there not ambition, ruthless competition? So the world is already in chaos, that is the first thing to realize. Don't take it for granted that this is an orderly society; don't mesmerize yourself with words. Whether, here in Europe, in America or Russia, the world is in a process of decay. If you see the decay, you have a challenge: you are challenged to find a way of solving this urgent problem. And how you respond to the challenge is important, is it not? If you respond as a Hindu or a Buddhist, a Christian or a communist, then your response is very limited—which is no response at all. You can respond fully, adequately only if there is no fear in you, only if you don't think as a Hindu, a communist or a capitalist, but as a total human being who is trying to solve this problem; and you cannot solve it unless you yourself are in revolt against the whole thing, against the ambitious acquisitiveness on which society is based. When you yourself are not ambitious, not acquisitive, not clinging to your own security—only then can you respond to the challenge and create a new world.

Questioner: To revolt, to learn, to love—are these three separate processes, or are they simultaneous?

KRISHNAMURTI: Of course they are not three separate processes; it is a unitary process. You see, it is very important to find out what the question means. This question is based on theory, not on experience; it is merely verbal, intellectual, therefore it has no validity. A man who is fearless, who is really in revolt, struggling to find out what it means to learn, to love—such a man does not ask if it is one process or three. We are so clever with words, and we think that by offering explanations we have solved the problem.

Do you know what it means to learn? When you are really learning you are learning throughout your life and there is no one special teacher to learn from. Then everything teaches you—a dead leaf, a bird in flight, a smell, a tear, the rich and the poor, those who are crying, the smile of a woman, the haughtiness of a man. You learn from everything, therefore there is no guide, no philosopher, no guru. Life itself is your teacher, and you are in a state of constant learning.

Questioner: Is it true that society is based on acquisitiveness and ambition; but if we had no ambition would we not decay?

KRISHNAMURTI: This is really a very important question, and it needs great attention.

Do you know what attention is? Let us find out. In a class room, when you stare out of the window or pull somebody's hair, the teacher tells you to pay attention. Which means what? That you are not interested in what you are studying and so the teacher compels you to pay attention—which is not attention at all. Attention comes when you are deeply interested in something, for then you love to find out all about it; then your whole mind, your whole being is there. Similarly, the moment you see that this question—if we had no ambition, would we not decay?—is really very important, you are interested and want to find out the truth of the matter.

Now, is not the ambitious man destroying himself? That is the first thing to find out, not to ask whether ambition is right or wrong. Look around you, observe all the people who are ambitious. What happens when you are ambitious? You are thinking about yourself, are you not? You are cruel, you push other people aside because you are trying to fulfil your ambition, trying to become a big man, thereby creating in society the conflict between those who are succeeding and those who are falling behind. There is a constant battle between you and the others who are also after what you want; and is this conflict productive of creative living? Do you understand, or is this too difficult?

Are you ambitious when you love to do something for its own sake? When you are doing something with your whole being, not because you want to get somewhere, or have more profit, or greater results, but simply because you love to do it—in that there is no ambition, is there? In that there is no competition; you are not struggling with anyone for first place. And should not education help you to find out what you really love to do so that from the beginning to the end of your life you are working at something which you feel is worth while and which for you has deep significance? Otherwise, for the rest of your days, you will be miserable. Not knowing what you really want to do, your mind falls into a routine in which there is only boredom, decay and death. That is why it is very important to find out while you are young what it is you really *love* to do; and this is the only way to create a new society.

Questioner: In India, as in most other countries, education is being controlled by the government. Under such circumstances is it possible to carry out an experiment of the kind you describe?

KRISHNAMURTI: If there were no government help, would it be possible for a school of this kind to survive? That is what this gentleman is asking. He sees everything throughout the world becoming more and more controlled by governments, by politicians, by people in authority who want to shape our minds and hearts, who want us to think in a certain way. Whether in Russia or in any other country, the tendency is towards government control of education; and this gentlemen asks whether it is possible for a school of the kind I am talking about to come into being without government aid.

Now, what do *you* say? You know, if you think something is important, really worth while, you give your heart to it irrespective of governments and the edicts of society—and then it will succeed. But most of us do not give our hearts to anything, and that is why we put this sort of question. If you and I feel vitally that a new world can be brought into being, when each one of us is in complete revolt inwardly, psychologically, spiritually—then we shall give our hearts, our minds, our bodies towards creating a school where there is no such thing as fear with all its implications.

Sir, anything truly revolutionary is created by a few who see what is true and are willing to live according to that truth; but to discover what is true demands freedom from tradition, which means freedom from all fears.

2

The Problem of Freedom

I would like to discuss with you the problem of freedom. It is a very complex problem, needing deep study and understanding. We hear much talk about freedom, religious freedom, and the freedom to do what one would like to do. Volumes have been written on all this by scholars. But I think we can approach it very simply and directly, and perhaps that will bring us to the real solution.

I wonder if you have ever stopped to observe the marvellous glow in the west as the sun sets, with the shy young moon just over the trees? Often at that hour the river is very calm, and then everything is reflected on its surface: the bridge, the train that goes over it, the tender moon, and presently, as it grows dark, the stars. It is all very beautiful. And to observe, to watch, to give your whole attention to something beautiful, your mind must be free of preoccupations, must it not? It must not be occupied with problems, with worries, with speculations. It is only when the mind is very quiet that you can really observe, for then the mind is sensitive to extraordinary beauty; and perhaps here is a clue to our problem of freedom.

Now, what does it mean to be free? Is freedom a matter of doing what happens to suit you, going where you like, thinking what you will? This you do anyhow.

Merely to have independence, does that mean freedom? Many people in the world are independent, but very few are free. Freedom implies great intelligence, does it not? To be free is to be intelligent, but intelligence does not come into being by just wishing to be free; it comes into being only when you begin to understand your whole environment, the social, religious, parental and traditional influences that are continually closing in on you. But to understand the various influences—the influence of your parents, of your government, of society, of the culture to which you belong, of your beliefs, your gods and superstitions, of the tradition to which you conform unthinkingly—to understand all these and become free from them requires deep insight; but you generally give in to them because inwardly you are frightened. You are afraid of not having a good position in life; you are afraid of what your priest will say; you are afraid of not following tradition, of not doing the right thing. But freedom is really a state of mind in which there is no fear or compulsion, no urge to be secure.

Don't most of us want to be safe? Don't we want to be told what marvellous people we are, how lovely we look, or what extraordinary intelligence we have? Otherwise we would not put letters after our names. All that kind of thing gives us self-assurance, a sense of importance. We all want to be famous people—and the moment we want to *be* something, we are no longer free.

Please see this, for it is the real clue to the understanding of the problem of freedom. Whether in this world of politicians, power, position and authority, or in the so-called spiritual world where you aspire to be virtuous, noble, saintly, the moment you want to be somebody you are no longer free. But the man or the woman who sees the absurdity of all these things and whose heart is therefore innocent, and therefore not moved by the desire to be somebody—such a person is free. If you understand the simplicity of it you will also see its extraordinary beauty and depth.

After all, examinations are for that purpose: to give you a position, to make you somebody. Titles, position and knowledge encourage you to be something. Have you not noticed that your parents and teachers tell you that you must amount to something in life, that you must be successful like your uncle or your grandfather? Or you try to imitate the example of some hero, to be like the Masters, the saints; so you are never free. Whether you follow the example of a Master, a saint, a teacher, a relative, or stick to a particular tradition, it all implies a demand on your part to *be* something; and it is only when you really understand this fact that there is freedom.

The function of education, then, is to help you from childhood not to imitate anybody, but to be yourself all the time. And this is a most difficult thing to do: whether you are ugly or beautiful, whether you are envious or jealous, always to be what you are, but understand it. To be yourself is very difficult, because you think that what you are is ignoble, and that if you could only change what you are into something noble it would be marvellous; but that never happens. Whereas, if you look at what you actually are and understand it, then in that very understanding there is a transformation. So freedom lies, not in trying to become something different, nor in doing whatever you happen to feel like doing, nor in following the authority of tradition, of your parents, of your *guru*, but in understanding what you are from moment to moment.

You see, you are not educated for this; your education encourages you to become something or other—but that is not the understanding of yourself. Your "self" is a very complex thing; it is not merely the entity that goes to school, that quarrels, that plays games, that is afraid, but it is aslo something hidden, not obvious. It is made up, not only of all the thoughts that you think, but also of all the things that have been put into your mind by other people, by books, by the newspapers, by your leaders; and it is possible to understand all that only when you don't want to be somebody, when you don't imitate, when you don't follow—which means, really, when you are in revolt against the whole tradition of trying to become something. That is the only true revolution, leading to extraordinary freedom. To cultivate this freedom is the real function of education.

Your parents, your teachers and your own desires want you to be identified with something or other in order to be happy, secure. But to be intelligent, must you not break through all the influences that enslave and crush you?

The hope of a new world is in those of you who begin to see what is false and revolt against it, not just verbally but actually. And that is why you should seek the right kind of education; for it is only when you grow in freedom that you can create a new world not based on tradition or shaped according to the idiosyncrasy of some philosopher or idealist. But there can be no freedom as long as you are merely trying to become somebody, or imitate a noble example.

Questioner: What is intelligence?

KRISHNAMURTI: Let us go into the question very slowly, patiently, and find out. To find out is not to come to a conclusion. I don't know if you see the difference. The moment you come to a conclusion as to what intelligence is, you cease to be intelligent. That is what most of the older people have done: they have come to conclusions. Therefore they have ceased to be intelligent. So you have found out one thing right off: that an intelligent mind is one which is constantly learning, never concluding.

What is intelligence? Most people are satisfied with a definition of what intelligence is. Either they say, "That is a good explanation," or they prefer their own explanation; and a mind that is satisfied with an explanation is very superficial, therefore it is not intelligent.

You have begun to see that an intelligent mind is a mind which is not satisfied with explanations, with conclusions; nor is it a mind that believes, because belief is again another form of conclusion. An intelligent mind is an inquiring mind, a mind that is watching, learning, studying. Which means what? That there is intelligence only when there is no fear, when you are willing to rebel, to go against the whole social structure in order to find out what God is, or to discover the truth of anything.

Intelligence is not knowledge. If you could read all the books in the world it would not give you intelligence. Intelligence is something very subtle; it has no anchorage. It comes into being only when you understand the total process of the mind—not the mind according to some philosopher or teacher, but your own mind. Your mind is the result of all humanity, and when you understand it you don't have to study a single book, because the mind contains the whole knowledge of the past. So intelligence comes into being with the understanding of yourself; and you can understand yourself only in relation to the world of people, things and ideas. Intelligence is not something that you can acquire, like learning; it arises with great revolt, that is, when there is no fear—which means, really, when there is a sense of love. For when there is no fear, there is love.

If you are only interested in explanations, I am afraid you will feel that I have not answered your question. To ask what is intelligence is like asking what is life. Life is study, play, sex, work, quarrel, envy, ambition, love, beauty, truth—life is everything, is it not? But you see, most of us have not the patience earnestly and consistently to pursue this inquiry.

Questioner: Can the crude mind become sensitive?

KRISHNAMURTI: Listen to the question, to the meaning behind the words. Can the crude mind become sensitive? If I say my mind is crude and I try to become sensitive, the very effort to become sensitive is crudity. Please see this. Don't be intrigued, but watch it. Whereas, if I recognize that I am crude without wanting to change, without trying to become sensitive, if I begin to understand what crudeness is, observe it in my life from day to day —the greedy way I eat, the roughness with which I treat people, the pride, the arrogance, the coarseness of my habits and thoughts—then that very observation transforms what *is*.

Similarly, if I am stupid and I say I must become intelligent, the effort to become intelligent is only a greater form of stupidity; because what is important is to understand stupidity. However much I may try to become intelligent, my stupidity will remain. I may acquire the superficial polish of learning, I may be able to quote books, repeat passages from great authors, but basically I shall still be stupid. But if I see and understand stupidity as it expresses itself in my daily life—how I behave towards my servant, how I regard my neighbour, the poor man, the rich man, the clerk—then that very awareness brings about a breaking up of stupidity.

You try it. Watch yourself talking to your servant, observe the tremendous respect with which you treat a governor, and how little respect you show to the man who has nothing to give you. Then you begin to find out how stupid you are; and in understanding that stupidity there is intelligence, sensitivity. You do not have to *become* sensitive. The man who is trying to become something is ugly, insensitive; he is a crude person.

Questioner: How can the child find out what he is without the help of his parents and teachers?

KRISHNAMURTI: Have I said that he can, or is this your interpretation of what I said? The child will find out about himself if the environment in which he lives helps him to do so. If the parents and teachers are really concerned that the young person should discover what he is, they won't compel him; they will create an environment in which he will come to know himself.

You have asked this question; but is it a vital problem to you? If you deeply felt that it is important for the child to find out about himself, and that he cannot do this if he is dominated by authority, would you not help to bring about the right environment? It is again the same old attitude: tell me what to do and I will do it. We don't say, "Let us work it out together." This problem of how to create an environment in which the child can have knowledge of himself is one that concerns everybody—the parents, the teachers and the children themselves. But self-knowledge cannot be imposed, understanding cannot be compelled; and if this is a vital problem to you and me, to the parent and the teacher, then together we shall create schools of the right kind.

Questioner: The children tell me that they have seen in the villages some weird phenomena, like obsession, and that they are afraid of ghosts, spirits, and so on. They also ask about death. What is one to say to all this?

KRISHNAMURTI: In due course we shall inquire into what death is. But you see, fear is an extraordinary thing. You children have been told about ghosts by your parents, by older people, otherwise you would probably not see ghosts. Somebody has told you about obsession. You are too young to know about these things. It is not your own experience, it is the reflection of what older people have told you. And the older people themselves often know nothing about all this. They have merely read about it in some book, and think they have understood it. That brings up quite a different question: is there an experience which is uncontaminated by the past? If an experience is contaminated by the past it is merely a continuity of the past, and therefore not an original experience.

What is important is that those of you who are dealing with children should not impose upon them your own fallacies, your own notions about ghosts, your own particular ideas and experiences. This is a very difficult thing to avoid, because older people talk a great deal about all these inessential things that have no importance in life; so gradually they communicate to the children their own anxieties, fears and superstitions, and the children naturally repeat what they have heard. It is important that the older people, who generally know nothing about these things for themselves, do not talk about them in front of children, but instead help to create an atmosphere in which the children can grow in freedom and without fear.

3

Freedom and Love

Perhaps some of you do not wholly understand all that I have been saying about freedom; but, as I have pointed out, it is very important to be exposed to new ideas, to something to which you may not be accustomed. It is good to see what is beautiful, but you must also observe the ugly things of life, you must be awake to everything. Similarly, you must be exposed to things which you perhaps don't quite understand, for the more you think and ponder over these matters which may be somewhat difficult for you, the greater will be your capacity to live richly.

I don't know if any of you have noticed, early in the morning, the sunlight on the waters. How extraordinarily soft is the light, and how the dark waters dance, with the morning star over the trees, the only star in the sky. Do you ever notice any of that? Or are you so busy, so occupied with the daily routine, that you forget or have never known the rich beauty of this earth—this earth on which all of us have to live? Whether we call ourselves communists or capitalists, Hindus or Buddhists, Moslems or Christians, whether we are blind, lame, or well and happy, this earth is ours. Do you understand? It is our earth, not somebody else's; it is not only the rich man's earth, it does not belong exclusively to the powerful rulers, to the nobles of the land, but it is our earth, yours and mine. We are nobodies, yet we also live on this earth, and we all have to live together. It is the world of the poor as well as of the rich, of the unlettered as well as of the learned; it is *our* world, and I think it is very important to feel this and to love the earth, not just occasionally on a peaceful morning, but all the time. We can feel that it is our world and love it only when we understand what freedom is.

There is no such thing as freedom at the present time, we don't know what it means. We would like to be free but, if you notice, everybody—the teacher, the parent, the lawyer, the policeman, the soldier, the politician, the business man—is doing something in his own little corner to prevent that freedom. To be free is not merely to do what you like, or to break away from outward circumstances which bind you, but to understand the whole problem of dependence. Do you know what dependence is? You depend on your parents, don't you? You depend on your teachers, you depend on the cook, on the postman, on the man who brings you milk, and so on. That kind of dependence one can understand fairly easily. But there is a far deeper kind of dependence which one must understand before one can be free: the dependence on another for one's happiness. Do you know what it means to depend on somebody for your happiness? It is not the mere physical dependence on another which is so binding, but the inward, psychological dependence from which you derive so-called happiness; for when you depend on somebody in that way, you become a slave. If, as you grow older, you depend emotionally on your parents, on your wife or husband, on a *guru*, or on some idea, there is already the beginning of bondage. We don't understand this—although most of us, especially when we are young, want to be free.

To be free we have to revolt against all inward dependence, and we cannot revolt if we don't understand why we are dependent. Until we understand and really break away from all inward dependence we can never be free, for only in that understanding can there be freedom. But freedom is not a mere reaction. Do you know what a reaction is? If I say something that hurts you, if I call you an ugly name and you get angry with me, that is a reaction—a reaction born of dependence; and independence is a further reaction. But freedom is not a reaction, and until we understand reaction and go beyond it, we are never free.

Do you know what it means to love somebody? Do you know what it means to love a tree, or a bird, or a pet animal, so that you take care of it, feed it, cherish it, though it may give you nothing in return, though it may not offer you shade, or follow you, or depend on you? Most of us don't love in that way, we don't know what that means at all because our love is always hedged about with anxiety, jealousy, fear—which implies that we depend inwardly on another, we want to be loved. We don't just love and leave it there, but we ask something in return; and in that very asking we become dependent.

So freedom and love go together. Love is not a reaction. If I love you because you love me, that is mere trade, a thing to be bought in the market; it is not love. To love is not to ask anything in return, not even to feel that you are giving something—and it is only such love that can know freedom. But, you see, you are not educated for this. You are educated in mathematics, in chemistry, geography, history, and there it ends, because your parents' only concern is to help you get a good job and be successful in life. If they have money they may send you abroad, but like the rest of the world their whole purpose is that you should be rich and have a respectable position in society; and the higher you climb the more misery you cause for others, because to get there you have to compete, be ruthless. So parents send their children to schools where there is ambition, competition, where there is no love at all, and that is why a society such as ours is continually decaying, in constant strife; and though the politicians, the judges, the so-called nobles of the land talk about peace, it does not mean a thing.

Now, you and I have to understand this whole problem of freedom. We must find out for ourselves what it means to love; because if we don't love we can never be thoughtful, attentive; we can never be considerate. Do you know what it means to be considerate? When you see a sharp stone on a path trodden by many bare feet, you remove it, not because you have been asked, but because you feel for another—it does not matter who he is, and you may never meet him. To plant a tree and cherish it, to look at the river and enjoy the fullness of the earth, to observe a bird on the wing and see the beauty of its flight, to have sensitivity and be open to this extraordinary movement called life—for all this there must be freedom; and to be free you must love. Without love there is no freedom; without love, freedom is merely an idea which has no value at all. So it is only for those who understand and break away from inner dependence, and who therefore know what love is, that there can be freedom; and it is they alone who will bring about a new civilization, a different world.

Questioner: What is the origin of desire, and how can I get rid of it?

KRISHNAMURTI: It is a young man who is asking this question; and why should he get rid of desire? Do you understand? He is a young man, full of life, vitality;

why should he get rid of desire? He has been told that to be free of desire is one of the greatest virtues, and that through freedom from desire he will realize God, or whatever that ultimate something may be called; so he asks, "What is the origin of desire, and how can I get rid of it?" But the very urge to get rid of desire is still part of desire, is it not? It is really prompted by fear.

What is the origin, the source, the beginning of desire? You see something attractive and you want it. You see a car, or a boat, and you want to possess it; or you want to achieve the position of a rich man, or become a *sannyasi*. This is the origin of desire: seeing, contacting, from which there is sensation, and from sensation there is desire. Now, recognizing that desire brings conflict, you ask, "How can I be free of desire?" So what you really want is not freedom from desire, but freedom from the worry, the anxiety, the pain which desire causes. You want freedom from the bitter fruits of desire, not from desire itself, and this is a very important thing to understand. If you could strip desire of pain, of suffering, of struggle, of all the anxieties and fears that go with it, so that only the pleasure remained, would you then want to be free of desire?

As long as there is the desire to gain, to achieve, to become, at whatever level, there is inevitably anxiety, sorrow, fear. The ambition to be rich, to be this or that, drops away only when we see the rottenness, the corruptive nature of ambition itself. The moment we see that the desire for power in any form—for the power of a prime minister, of a judge, of a priest, of a *guru*—is fundamentally evil, we no longer have the desire to be powerful. But we don't see that ambition is corrupting, that the desire for power is evil; on the contrary, we say that we shall use power for good—which is all nonsense. A wrong means can never be used towards a right end.

If the means is evil, the end will also be evil. Good is not the opposite of evil; it comes into being only when that which is evil has utterly ceased.

So, if we don't understand the whole significance of desire, with its results, its by-products, merely to try to get rid of desire has no meaning.

Questioner: How can we be free of dependence as long as we are living in society?

KRISHNAMURTI: Do you know what society is? Society is the relationship between man and man, is it not? Don't complicate it, don't quote a lot of books; think very simply about it and you will see that society is the relationship between you and me and others. Human relationship makes society; and our present society is built upon a relationship of acquisitiveness, is it not? Most of us want money, power, property, authority; at one level or another we want position, prestige, and so we have built an acquisitive society. As long as we are acquisitive, as long as we want position, prestige, power and all the rest of it, we belong to this society and are therefore dependent on it. But if one does not want any of these things and remains simply what one is with great humility, then one is out of it; one revolts against it and breaks with this society.

Unfortunately, education at present is aimed at making you conform, fit into and adjust yourself to this acquisitive society. That is all your parents, your teachers and your books are concerned with. As long as you conform, as long as you are ambitious, acquisitive, corrupting and destroying others in the pursuit of position and power, you are considered a respectable citizen. You are educated to fit into society; but that is not education, it is merely a process which conditions you to conform to a pattern. The real function of education is not to turn you out to be a clerk, or a judge, or a prime minister, but to help you understand the whole structure of this rotten society and allow you to grow to freedom, so that you will break away and create a different society, a new world. There must be those who are in revolt, not partially but totally in revolt against the old, for it is only such people who can create a new world—a world not based on acquisitiveness, on power and prestige.

I can hear the older people saying, "It can never be done. Human nature is what it is, and you are talking nonsense." But we have never thought about unconditioning the adult mind, and not conditioning the child. Surely, education is both curative and preventive. You older students are already shaped, already conditioned, already ambitious; you want to be successful like your father, like the governor, or somebody else. So the real function of education is not only to help you uncondition yourself, but also to understand this whole process of living from day to day so that you can grow in freedom and create a new world—a world that must be totally different from the present one. Unfortunately, neither your parents, nor your teachers, nor the public in general are interested in this. That is why education must be a process of educating the educator as well as the student.

Questioner: Why do men fight?

KRISHNAMURTI: Why do young boys fight? You sometimes fight with your brother, or with the other boys here, don't you? Why? You fight over a toy. Perhaps another boy has taken your ball, or your book, and therefore you fight. Grown-up people fight for exactly the same reason, only their toys are position, wealth and power. If you want power and I also want power, we fight, and that is why nations go to war. It is as simple as that, only philosophers, politicians and the so-called religious people complicate it. You know, it is a great art to have an abundance of knowledge and experience—to know the richness of life, the beauty of existence, the struggles, the miseries, the laughter, the tears—and yet keep your mind very simple; and you can have a simple mind only when you know how to love.

Questioner: What is jealousy?

KRISHNAMURTI: Jealousy implies dissatisfaction with what you are and envy of others, does it not? To be discontented with what you are is the very beginning of envy. You want to be like somebody else who has more knowledge, or is more beautiful, or who has a bigger house, more power, a better position than you have. You want to be more virtuous, you want to know how to meditate better, you want to reach God, you want to be something different from what you are; therefore you are envious, jealous. To understand what you are is immensely difficult, because it requires complete freedom from all desire to change what you are into something else. The desire to change yourself breeds envy, jealousy; whereas, in the understanding of what you are, there is a transformation of what you are. But, you see, your whole education urges you to try to be different from what you are. When you are jealous you are told, "Now, don't be jealous, it is a terrible thing." So you strive not to be jealous; but that very striving is part of jealousy, because you want to be different.

You know, a lovely rose is a lovely rose; but we human beings have been given the capacity to think, and we think wrongly. To know *how* to think requires a a great deal of penetration, understanding, but to know *what* to think is comparatively easy. Our present education consists in telling us *what* to think, it does not teach us *how* to think, how to penetrate, explore; and it is only when the teacher as well as the student knows how to think that the school is worthy of its name.

Questioner: Why am I never satisfied with anything?

KRISHNAMURTI: A little girl is asking this question, and I am sure she has not been prompted. At her tender age she wants to know why she is never satisfied. What do you grown-up people say? It is your doing; you have brought into existence this world in which a little girl asks why she is never satisfied with anything. You are supposed to be educators, but you don't see the tragedy of this. You meditate, but you are dull, weary, inwardly dead.

Why are human beings never satisfied? Is it not because they are seeking happiness, and they think that through constant change they will be happy? They move from one job to another, from one relationship to another, from one religion or ideology to another, thinking that through this constant movement of change they will find happiness; or else they choose some backwater of life and stagnate there. Surely, contentment is something entirely different. It comes into being only when you see yourself as you are without any desire to change, without any condemnation or comparison—which does not mean that you merely accept what you see and go to sleep. But when the mind is no longer comparing, judging, evaluating, and is therefore capable of seeing what *is* from moment to moment without wanting to change it—in that very perception is the eternal.

Questioner: Why must we read?

KRISHNAMURTI: Why must you read? Just listen quietly. You never ask why you must play, why you must eat, why you must look at the river, why you are cruel—do you? You rebel and ask why you must do something when you don't like to do it. But reading, playing, laughing, being cruel, being good, seeing the river, the clouds—all this is part of life; and if you don't know how to read, if you don't know how to walk, if you are unable to appreciate the beauty of a leaf, you are not living. You must understand the whole of life, not just one little part of it. That is why you must read, that is why you must look at the skies, that is why you must sing, and dance, and write poems, and suffer, and understand; for all that is life.

Questioner: What is shyness?

KRISHNAMURTI: Don't you feel shy when you meet a stranger? Didn't you feel shy when you asked that question? Wouldn't you feel shy if you had to be on this platform, as I am, and sit here talking? Don't you feel shy, don't you feel a bit awkward and want to stand still when you suddenly come upon a lovely tree, or a delicate flower, or a bird sitting on its nest? You see, it is good to be shy. But for most of us shyness implies self-consciousness. When we meet a big man, if there is such a person, we become conscious of ourselves. We think, "How important he is, so well known, and I am nobody"; so we feel shy, which is to be conscious of oneself. But there is a different kind of shyness, which is really to be tender, and in that there is no self-consciousness.

4
Listening

Why are you here listening to me? Have you ever considered why you listen to people at all? And what does listening to somebody mean? All of you here are sitting in front of one who is speaking. Are you listening to hear something that will confirm, tally with your own thoughts, or are you listening to find out? Do you see the difference? Listening to find out has quite a different significance from listening merely to hear that which will confirm what you think. If you are here merely to have confirmation, to be encouraged in your own thinking, then your listening has very little meaning. But, if you are listening to find out, then your mind is free, not committed to anything; it is very acute, sharp, alive, inquiring, curious, and therefore capable of discovery. So, is it not very important to consider why you listen, and what you are listening to?

Have you ever sat very silently, not with your attention fixed on anything, not making an effort to concentrate, but with the mind very quiet, really still? Then you hear everything, don't you? You hear the far-off noises as well as those that are nearer and those that are very close by, the immediate sounds—which means, really, that you are listening to everything. Your mind is not confined to one narrow little channel. If you can listen in this way, listen with ease, without strain, you will find an extraordinary change taking place within you, a change which comes without your volition, without your asking; and in that change there is great beauty and depth of insight.

Just try it sometime, try it now. As you are listening to me, listen not only to me, but to everything about you. Listen to all those bells, the bells of the cows and the temples; listen to the distant train and the carts on the road; and if you then come nearer still and listen to me also, you will find there is a great depth to listening. But to do this you must have a very quiet mind. If you really want to listen, your mind is naturally quiet, is it not? You are not then distracted by something happening next to you; your mind is quiet because you are deeply listening to everything. If you can listen in this way with ease, with a certain felicity, you will find an astonishing transformation taking place in your heart, in your mind—a transformation which you have not thought of, or in any way produced.

Thought is a very strange thing, is it not? Do you know what thought is? Thought or thinking for most people is something put together by the mind, and they battle over their thoughts. But if you can really listen to everything—to the lapping of the water on the bank of a river, to the song of the birds, to the crying of a child, to your mother scolding you, to a friend bullying you, to your wife or husband nagging you—then you will find that you go beyond the words, beyond the mere verbal expressions which so tear one's being.

And it is very important to go beyond the mere verbal expressions because, after all, what is it that we all want? Whether we are young or old, whether we are inexperienced or full of years, we all want to be happy, don't we? As students we want to be happy in playing our games, in studying, in doing all the little things we like to do. As we grow older we seek happiness in possessions, in money, in having a nice house, a sympathetic wife or husband, a good job. When these things no longer satisfy us, we move onto something else. We say, "I must be detached and then I shall be happy." So we begin to practise detachment. We leave our family, give up our property and retire from the world. Or we join some religious society, thinking that we shall be happy by getting together and talking about brotherhood, by following a leader, a *guru*, a Master, an ideal, by believing in what is essentially a self-deception, an illusion, a superstition.

Do you understand what I am talking about?

When you comb your hair, when you put on clean clothes and make yourself look nice, that is all part of your desire to be happy, is it not? When you pass your examinations and add a few letters of the alphabet after your name, when you get a job, acquire a house and other property, when you marry and have children, when you join some religious society whose leaders claim they have messages from unseen Masters—behind it all there is this extraordinary urge, this compulsion to find happiness.

But, you see, happiness does not come so easily, because happiness is in none of these things. You may have pleasure, you may find a new satisfaction, but sooner or later it becomes wearisome. Because there is no lasting happiness in the things we know. The kiss is followed by the tear, laughter by misery and desolation. Everything withers, decays. So, while you are young you must begin to find out what is this strange thing called happiness. That is an essential part of education.

Happiness does not come when you are striving for it—and that is the greatest secret, though it is very easily said. I can put it in a few simple words; but, by merely listening to me and repeating what you have heard, you are not going to be happy. Happiness is strange; it comes when you are not seeking it. When you are not making an effort to be happy, then unexpectedly, mysteriously happiness is there, born of purity, of a loveliness of being. But that requires a great deal of understanding—not joining an organization or trying to become somebody. Truth is not something to be achieved. Truth comes into being when your mind and heart are purged of all sense of striving and you are no longer trying to become somebody; it is there when the mind is very quiet, listening timelessly to everything that is happening. You may listen to these words but, for happiness to be, you have to find out how to free the mind of all fear.

As long as you are afraid of anyone or anything, there can be no happiness. There can be no happiness as long as you are afraid of your parents, your teachers, afraid of not passing examinations, afraid of not making progress, of not getting nearer to the Master, nearer to truth, or of not being approved of, patted on the back. But if you are really not afraid of anything, then you will find—when you wake up of a morning, or when you are walking alone—that suddenly a strange thing happens: uninvited, unsolicited, unlooked for, that which may be called love, truth, happiness, is suddenly there.

That is why it is so important for you to be educated rightly while you are young. What we now call education is not education at all, because nobody talks to you about all these things. Your teachers prepare you to pass examinations, but they do not talk to you about living, which is most important; because very few know how to live. Most of us merely survive, we somehow drag along, and therefore life becomes a dreadful thing. Really to live requires a great deal of love, a great feeling for silence, a great simplicity with an abundance of experience; it requires a mind that is capable of thinking very clearly, that is not bound by prejudice or superstition, by hope or fear. All this is life, and if you are not being educated to live, then education has no meaning. You may learn to be very tidy, have good manners, and you may pass all your examinations; but, to give primary importance to these superficial things when the whole structure of society is crumbling, is like cleaning and polishing your fingernails while the house is burning down. You see, nobody talks to you about all this, nobody goes into it with you. As you spend day after day studying certain subjects—mathematics, history, geography—so also you should spend a great deal of time talking about these deeper matters, because this makes for richness of life.

Questioner: Is not the worship of God true religion?

KRISHNAMURTI: First of all, let us find out what is *not* religion. Isn't that the right approach? If we can understand what is *not* religion, then perhaps we shall begin to perceive something else. It is like cleaning a dirty window—one begins to see through it very clearly. So let us see if we can understand and sweep out of our minds that which is not religion; don't let us say, "I will think about it" and just play around with words. Perhaps you can do it, but most of the older people are already caught; they are comfortably established in that which is not religion and they do not want to be disturbed.

So, what is not religion? Have you ever thought about it? You have been told over and over again what religion is supposed to be—belief in God and a dozen other things—but nobody has asked you to find out what is *not* religion and now you and I are going to find out for ourselves.

In listening to me, or to anyone else, do not merely accept what is said, but listen to discern the truth of the matter. If once you perceive for yourself what is not religion, then throughout your life no priest or book can deceive you, no sense of fear will create an illusion which you may believe and follow. To find out what is not religion you have to begin on the everyday level, and then you can climb. To go far you must begin near, and the nearest step is the most important one. So, what is not religion? Are ceremonies religion? Doing *puja* over and over again—is that religion?

True education is to learn *how* to think, not *what* to think. If you know how to think, if you really have that capacity, then you are a free human being—free of dogmas, superstitions, ceremonies—and therefore you can find out what religion is.

Ceremonies are obviously not religion, because in performing ceremonies you are merely repeating a formula which has been handed down to you. You may find a certain pleasure in performing ceremonies, just as others do in smoking or drinking; but is that religion? In performing ceremonies you are doing something about which you know nothing. Your father and your grandfather do it, therefore you do it, and if you don't they will scold you. That is not religion, is it?

And what is in a temple? A graven image fashioned by a human being according to his own imagination. The image may be a symbol, but it is still only an image, it is not the real thing. A symbol, a word, is not the thing it represents. The word 'door' is not the door, is it? The word is not the thing. We go to the temple to worship—what? An image which is supposed to be a symbol; but the symbol is not the real thing. So why go to it? These are facts; I am not condemning; and, since they are facts, why bother about who goes to the temple, whether it be the touchable or the untouchable, the brahman or the non-brahman? Who cares? You see, the older people have made the symbol into a religion for which they are willing to quarrel, fight, slaughter; but God is not there.

God is never in a symbol. So the worship of a symbol or of an image is not religion.

And is belief religion? This is more complex. We began near, and now we are going a little bit farther. Is belief religion? The Christians believe in one way, the Hindus in another, the Moslems in another, the Buddhists in still another, and they all consider themselves very religious people; they all have their temples, gods, symbols, beliefs. And is that religion? Is it religion when you believe in God, in Rama, Sita, Ishwara, and all that kind of thing? How do you get such a belief? You believe because your father and your grandfather believe; or having read what some teacher like Shankara or Buddha is supposed to have said, you believe it and say it is true. Most of you just believe what the *Gita* says, therefore you don't examine it clearly and simply as you would any other book; you don't try to find out what is true.

We have seen that ceremonies are not religion, that going to a temple is not religion, and that belief is not religion. Belief divides people. The Christians have beliefs and so are divided both from those of other beliefs and among themselves; the Hindus are everlastingly full of enmity because they believe themselves to be brahmans or non-brahmans, this or that. So belief brings enmity, division, destruction, and that is obviously not religion.

Then what *is* religion? If you have wiped the window clean—which means that you have actually stopped performing ceremonies, given up all beliefs, ceased to follow any leader or *guru*—then your mind, like the window, is clean, polished, and you can see out of it very clearly. When the mind is swept clean of image, of ritual, of belief, of symbol, of all words, *mantrams* and repetitions, and of all fear, then what you see will be the real, the timeless, the everlasting, which may be called

God; but this requires enormous insight, understanding, patience, and it is only for those who really inquire into what is religion and pursue it day after day to the end. Only such people will know what is true religion. The rest are merely mouthing words, and all their ornaments and bodily decorations, their *pujas* and ringing of bells—all that is just superstition without any significance. It is only when the mind is in revolt against all so-called religion that it finds the real.

5

Creative Discontent

Have you ever sat very quietly without any movement? You try it, sit really still, with your back straight, and observe what your mind is doing. Don't try to control it, don't say it should not jump from one thought to another, from one interest to another, but just be aware of how your mind is jumping. Don't do anything about it, but watch it as from the banks of a river you watch the water flow by. In the flowing river there are so many things—fishes, leaves, dead animals—but it is always living, moving, and your mind is like that. It is everlastingly restless, flitting from one thing to another like a butterfly.

When you listen to a song, how do you listen to it? You may like the person who is singing, he may have a nice face, and you may follow the meaning of the words; but behind all that, when you listen to a song, you are listening to the tones and to the silence between the tones, are you not? In the same way, try sitting very quietly without fidgeting, without moving your hands or even your toes, and just watch your mind. It is great fun. If you try it as fun, as an amusing thing, you will find that the mind begins to settle down without any effort on your part to control it. There is then no censor, no judge, no evaluator; and when the mind is thus very quiet of itself, spontaneously still, you will discover what it is to be gay. Do you know what gaiety is? It is just to laugh, to take delight in anything or nothing, to know the joy of living, smiling, looking straight into the face of another without any sense of fear.

Have you ever really looked anybody in the face? Have you ever looked into the face of your teacher, of your parent, of the big official, of the servant, the poor *coolie,* and seen what happens? Most of us are afraid to look directly into the face of another; and others don't want us to look at them in that way, because they also are frightened. Nobody wants to reveal himself; we are all on guard, hiding behind various layers of misery, suffering, longing, hope, and there are very few who can look you straight in the face and smile. And it is very important to smile, to be happy; because, you see, without a song in one's heart life becomes very dull. One may go from temple to temple, from one husband or wife to another, or one may find a new teacher or *guru;* but if there is not this inward joy, life has very little meaning. And to find this inward joy is not easy, because most of us are only superficially discontented.

Do you know what it means to be discontented? It is very difficult to understand discontent, because most of us canalize discontent in a certain direction and thereby smother it. That is, our only concern is to establish ourselves in a secure position with well-established interests and prestige, so as not to be disturbed. It happens in homes and in schools too. The teachers don't want to be disturbed, and that is why they follow the old routine; because the moment one is really discontented and begins to inquire, to question, there is bound to be disturbance. But it is only through real discontent that one has initiative.

Do you know what initiative is? You have initiative when you initiate or start something without being prompted. It need not be anything very great or extraordinary—that may come later; but there is the spark of initiative when you plant a tree on your own, when you are spontaneously kind, when you smile at a man who is carrying a heavy load, when you remove a stone from the path, or pat an animal along the way. That is a small beginning of the tremendous initiative you must have if you are to know this extraordinary thing called creativeness. Creativeness has its roots in the initiative which comes into being only when there is deep discontent.

Don't be afraid of discontent, but give it nourishment until the spark becomes a flame and you are everlastingly discontented with everything—with your jobs, with your families, with the traditional pursuit of money, position, power—so that you really begin to think, to discover. But as you grow older you will find that to maintain this spirit of discontent is very difficult. You have children to provide for and the demands of your job to consider; the opinion of your neighbours, of society closing in upon you, and soon you begin to lose this burning flame of discontent. When you feel discontented you turn on the radio, you go to a *guru*, do *puja*, join a club, drink, run after women—anything to smother the flame. But, you see, without this flame of discontent you will never have the initiative which is the beginning of creativeness. To find out what is true you must be in revolt against the established order; but the more money your parents have, and the more secure your teachers are in their jobs, the less they want you to revolt.

Creativeness is not merely a matter of painting pictures or writing poems, which is good to do, but which is very little in itself. What is important is to be wholly discontented, for such total discontent is the beginning of the initiative which becomes creative as it matures; and that is the only way to find out what is truth, what is God, because the creative state is God.

So one must have this total discontent—but with joy.

Do you understand? One must be wholly discontented, not complainingly, but with joy, with gaiety, with love. Most people who are discontented are terrible bores; they are always complaining that something or other is not right, or wishing they were in a better position, or wanting circumstances to be different, because their discontent is very superficial. And those who are not discontented at all are already dead.

If you can be in revolt while you are young, and as you grow older keep your discontent alive with the vitality of joy and great affection, then that flame of discontent will have an extraordinary significance because it will build, it will create, it will bring new things into being. For this you must have the right kind of education, which is not the kind that merely prepares you to get a job or to climb the ladder of success, but the education that helps you to think and gives you space—space, not in the form of a larger bedroom or a higher roof, but space for your mind to grow so that it is not bound by any belief, by any fear.

Questioner: Discontent prevents clear thinking. How are we to overcome this obstacle?

KRISHNAMURTI: I don't think you can have listened to what I was saying; probably you were concerned with your question, worrying about how you were going to put it. That is what you are all doing in different ways. Each one has a preoccupation, and if what I say is not what you want to hear you brush it aside because your mind is occupied with your own problem. If the questioner had listened to what was being said, if he had really felt the inward nature of discontent, of gaiety, of being creative, then I don't think he would have put this question.

Now, does discontent prevent clear thinking? And what is clear thinking? Is it possible to think very clearly if you want to get something out of your thinking? If your mind is concerned with a result, can you think very clearly? Or can you think very clearly only when you are not seeking an end, a result, not trying to gain something?

And can you think clearly if you have a prejudice, a particular belief—that is, if you think as a Hindu, a communist, or a Christian? Surely, you can think very clearly only when your mind is not tethered to a belief as a monkey might be tethered to a stake; you can think very clearly only when you are not seeking a result; you can think very clearly only when you have no prejudice—all of which means, really, that you can think clearly, simply and directly only when your mind is no longer pursuing any form of security and is therefore free of fear.

So, in one way, discontent *does* prevent clear thinking. When through discontent you pursue a result, or when you seek to smother discontent because your mind hates to be disturbed and wants at all costs to be quiet, peaceful, then clear thinking is not possible. But if you are discontented with everything—with your prejudices, with your beliefs, with your fears—and are not seeking a result, then that very discontent brings your thought into focus, not upon any particular object or in any particular direction, but your whole thinking process becomes very simple, direct and clear.

Young or old, most of us are discontented merely because we want something—more knowledge, a better job, a finer car, a bigger salary. Our discontent is based upon our desire for "the more." It is only because we want something more that most of us are discontented. But I am not talking about that kind of discontent. It is the desire for 'the more' that prevents clear thinking. Whereas, if we are discontented, not because we want somehing, but without knowing *what* we want; if we are dissatisfied with our jobs, with making money, with seeking position and power, with tradition, with what we have and with what we might have; if we are dissatisfied, not with anything in particular but with everything, then I think we shall find that our discontent brings clarity. When we don't accept or follow, but question, investigate, penetrate, there is an insight out of which comes creativity, joy.

Questioner: What is self-knowledge, and how can we get it?

KRISHNAMURTI: Do you see the mentality behind this question? I am not speaking out of disrespect for the questioner, but let us look at the mentality that asks, "How can I get it, for how much can I buy it? What must I do, what sacrifice must I make, what discipline or meditation must I practise in order to have it?" It is a machine-like, mediocre mind which says, "I shall do *this* in order to get *that*." The so-called religious people think in these terms; but self-knowledge is not come by in this way. You cannot buy it through some effort or practice. Self-knowledge comes when you observe yourself in your relationship with your fellow-students and your teachers, with all the people around you; it comes when you observe the manner of another, his gestures, the way he wears his clothes, the way he talks, his contempt or flattery and your response; it comes when you watch everything in you and about you and see yourself as you see your face in the mirror. When you look into the mirror you see yourself as you are, don't you? You may wish your head were a different shape, with a little more hair, and your face a little less ugly; but the fact is there, clearly reflected in the mirror, and you can't push it aside and say, "How beautiful I am!"

Now, if you can look into the mirror of relationship exactly as you look into the ordinary mirror, then there is no end to self-knowledge. It is like entering a fathomless ocean which has no shore. Most of us want to reach an end, we want to be able to say, "I have arrived at self-knowledge and I am happy"; but it is not like that at all. If you can look at yourself without condemning what you see, without comparing yourself with somebody else, without wishing to be more beautiful or more virtuous; if you can just observe what you are and move with it, then you will find that it is possible to go infinitely far. Then there is no end to the journey, and that is the mystery, the beauty of it.

Questioner: What is the soul?

KRISHNAMURTI: Our culture, our civilization has invented the word "soul"—civilization being the collective desire and will of many people. Look at the Indian civilization. Is it not the result of many people with their desires, their wills? Any civilization is the outcome of what may be called the collective will; and the collective will in this case has said that there must be something more than the physical body which dies, decays, something much greater, vaster, something indestructible, immortal; therefore it has established this idea of the soul. Now and then there may have been one or two people who have discovered for themselves something about this extraordinary thing called immortality, a state in which there is no death, and then all the mediocre minds have said, "Yes, that must be true, he must be right"; and because they want immortality they cling to the word "soul."

You also want to know if there is something more than mere physical existence, do you not? This ceaseless round of going to an office, working at something in which you have no vital interest, quarrelling, being envious, bearing children, gossiping with your neighbour, uttering useless words—you want to know if there is something more than all this. The very word "soul" embodies the idea of a state which is indestructible, timeless, does it not? But, you see, you never find out for yourself whether or not there is such a state. You don't say, "I am not concerned with what Christ, Shankara, or anybody else has said, nor with the dictates of tradition, of so-called civilization; I am going to find out for myself whether or not there is a state beyond the framework of time." You don't revolt against what civilization or the collective will has formulated; on the contrary, you accept it and say, "Yes, there is a soul." You call that formulation one thing, another calls it something else, and then you divide yourselves and become enemies over your conflicting beliefs.

The man who really wants to find out whether or not there is a state beyond the framework of time, must be free of civilization; that is, he must be free of the collective will and stand alone. And this is an essential part of education: to learn to stand alone so that you are not caught either in the will of the many or in the will of one, and are therefore capable of discovering for yourself what is true.

Don't depend on anybody. I or another may tell you there is a timeless state, but what value has that for you? If you are hungry you want to eat, and you don't want to be fed on mere words. What is important is for you to find out for yourself. You can see that everything about you is decaying, being destroyed. This so-called civilization is no longer being held together by the collective will; it is going to pieces. Life is challenging you from moment to moment, and if you merely respond to the challenge from the groove of habit, which is to respond in terms of acceptance, then your response has no validity. You can find out whether or not there is a timeless state, a state in which there is no movement of "the more" or of "the less," only when you say, "I am not going to accept, I am going to investigate, explore"—which means that you are not afraid to stand alone.

6

The Wholeness of Life

Most of us cling to some small part of life, and think that through that part we shall discover the whole. Without leaving the room we hope to explore the whole length and width of the river and perceive the richness of the green pastures along its banks. We live in a little room, we paint on a little canvas, thinking that we have grasped life by the hand or understood the significance of death; but we have not. To do that we must go outside. And it is extraordinarily difficult to go outside, to leave the room with its narrow window and see everything as it is without judging, without condemning, without saying, "This I like and that I don't like"; because most of us think that through the part we shall understand the whole. Through a single spoke we hope to understand the wheel; but one spoke does not make a wheel, does it? It takes many spokes, as well as a hub and a rim, to make the thing called a wheel, and we need to see the whole wheel in order to comprehend it. In the same way we must perceive the whole process of living if we are really to understand life.

I hope you are following all this, because education should help you to understand the whole of life and not just prepare you to get a job and carry on in the usual way with your marriage, your children, your insurance, your *pujas* and your little gods. But to bring about the right kind of education requires a great deal of intelligence, insight, and that is why it is so important for the educator himself to be educated to understand the whole process of life and not merely to teach you according to some formula, old or new.

Life is an extraordinary mystery—not the mystery in books, not the mystery that people talk about, but a mystery that one has to discover for oneself; and that is why it is so grave a matter that you should understand the little, the narrow, the petty, and go beyond it.

If you don't begin to understand life while you are young, you will grow up inwardly hideous; you will be dull, empty inside, though outwardly you may have money, ride in expensive cars, put on airs. That is why it is very important to leave your little room and perceive the whole expanse of the heavens. But you cannot do that unless you have love—not bodily love or divine love, but just love; which is to love the birds, the trees, the flowers, your teachers, your parents, and beyond your parents, humanity.

Will it not be a great tragedy if you don't discover for yourselves what it is to love? If you don't know love now, you will never know it, because as you grow older, what is called love will become something very ugly—a possession, a form of merchandise to be bought and sold. But if you begin now to have love in your heart, if you love the tree you plant, the stray animal you pat, then as you grow up you will not remain in your small room with its narrow window, but will leave it and love the whole of life.

Love is factual, it is not emotional, something to be cried over; it is not sentiment. Love has no sentimentality about it at all. And it is a very grave and important matter that you should know love while you are young. Your parents and teachers perhaps don't know love, and that is why they have created a terrible world, a society which is perpetually at war within itself and with other societies. Their religions, their philosophies and ideologies are all false because they have no love. They perceive only a part; they are looking out of a narrow window from which the view may be pleasant and extensive, but it is not the whole expanse of life. Without this feeling of intense love you can never have the perception of the whole; therefore you will always be miserable, and at the end of your life you will have nothing but ashes, a lot of empty words.

Questioner: Why do we want to be famous?

KRISHNAMURTI: Why do you think you want to be famous? I may explain; but, at the end of it, will you stop wanting to be famous? You want to be famous because everybody around you in this society wants to be famous. Your parents, your teachers, the *guru*, the *yogi*—they all want to be famous, well known, and so you do too.

Let us think this out together. Why do people want to be famous? First of all, it is profitable to be famous; and it gives you a great deal of pleasure, does it not? If you are known all over the world you feel very important, it gives you a sense of immortality. You want to be famous, you want to be known and talked about in the world because inside yourself you are nobody. Inwardly there is no richness, there is nothing there at all, therefore you want to be known in the world outside; but, if you are inwardly rich, then it does not matter to you whether you are known or unknown.

To be inwardly rich is much more arduous than to be outwardly rich and famous; it needs much more care, much closer attention. If you have a little talent and know how to exploit it, you become famous; but inward richness does not come about in that way. To be inwardly rich the mind has to understand and put away the things that are not important, like wanting to be famous. Inward richness implies standing alone; but the man who wants to be famous is afraid to stand alone because he depends on people's flattery and good opinion.

Questioner: When you were young you wrote a book in which you said: "These are not my words, they are the words of my Master." How is it that you now insist upon our thinking for ourselves? And who was your Master?

KRISHNAMURTI: One of the most difficult things in life is not to be bound by an idea; being bound is called being consistent. If you have the ideal of non-violence, you try to be consistent with that ideal. Now, the questioner is saying in effect, "You tell us to think for ourselves, which is contrary to what you said when you were a boy. Why are you not consistent?"

What does it mean to be consistent? This is really a very important point. To be consistent is to have a mind that is unvaryingly following a particular pattern of thinking—which means that you must not do contradictory things, one thing today and the opposite thing tomorrow. We are trying to find out what is a consistent mind. A mind which says, "I have taken a vow to be something and I am going to be that for the rest of my life" is called consistent; but it is really a most stupid mind, because it has come to a conclusion and it is living according to that conclusion. It is like a man building a wall around himself and letting life go by.

This is a very complex problem; I may be oversimplifying it, but I don't think so. When the mind is merely consistent it becomes mechanical and loses vitality, the glow, the beauty of free movement. It is functioning within a pattern. That is one part of the question.

The other is: who is the Master? You don't know the implications of all this. It is just as well. You see, it has been said that I wrote a certain book when I was a boy, and that gentleman has quoted from the book a statement which says that a Master helped to write it. Now, there are groups of people, like the Theosophists, who believe that there are Masters living in the remote Himalayas who guide and help the world; and that gentleman wants to know who the Master is. Listen carefully, because this applies to you also.

Does it matter very much who a Master or a *guru* is? What matters is life—not your *guru*, not a Master, a leader or a teacher who interprets life for you. It is *you* who have to understand life; it is *you* who are suffering, who are in misery; it is *you* who want to know the meaning of death, of birth, of meditation, of sorrow, and nobody can tell you. Others can explain, but their explanations may be entirely false, altogether wrong.

So it is good to be sceptical, because it gives you a chance to find out for yourself whether you need a *guru* at all. What is important is to be a light unto yourself, to be your own Master and disciple, to be both the teacher and the pupil. As long as you are learning, there is no teacher. It is only when you have stopped exploring, discovering, understanding the whole process of life, that the teacher comes into being—and such a teacher has no value. Then you are dead, and therefore your teacher is also dead.

Questioner: Why is man proud?

KRISHNAMURTI: Are you not proud if you write a nice hand, or when you win a game or pass some examination? Have you ever written a poem or painted a picture, and then shown it to a friend? If your friend says it is a lovely poem or a marvellous picture, don't you feel very pleased? When you have done something which somebody says is excellent, you feel a sense of pleasure, and that is all right, that is nice; but what happens the next time you paint a picture, or write a poem, or clean a room? You expect someone to come along and say what a wonderful boy you are; and, if no one comes, you no longer bother about painting, or writing, or cleaning. So you come to depend on the pleasure which others give you by their approbation. It is as simple as that. And then what happens? As you grow older you want what you do to be acknowledged by many people. You may say, "I will do this thing for the sake of my *guru*, for the sake of my country, for the sake of man, for the sake of God," but you are really doing it to gain recognition, out of which grows pride; and when you do anything in that way, it is not worth doing. I wonder if you understand all this?

To understand something like pride, you must be capable of thinking right through; you must see how it begins and the disaster it brings, see the whole of it, which means that you must be so keenly interested that your mind follows it to the end and does not stop half way. When you are really interested in a game you play it to the end, you don't suddenly stop in the middle and go home. But your mind is not used to this kind of thinking, and it is part of education to help you to inquire into the whole process of life and not just study a few subjects.

Questioner: As children we are told what is beautiful and what is ugly, with the result that all through life we go on repeating, "This is beautiful, that is ugly." How is one to know what is real beauty and what is ugliness?

KRISHNAMURTI: Suppose you say that a certain arch is beautiful, and someone else says it is ugly. Now, which is important: to fight over your conflicting opinions as to whether something is beautiful or ugly, or to be sensitive to both beauty and ugliness? In life there is filth, squalor, degradation, sorrow, tears, and there is also joy, laughter, the beauty of a flower in the sunlight. What matters, surely, is to be sensitive to everything, and not merely decide what is beautiful and what is ugly and remain with that opinion. If I say, "I am going to cultivate beauty and reject all ugliness," what happens? The cultivation of beauty then makes for insensitivity. It is like a man developing his right arm, making it very strong, and letting his left arm wither. So you must be awake to ugliness as well as to beauty. You must see the dancing leaves, the water flowing under the bridge, the beauty of an evening, and also be aware of the beggar in the street; you must see the poor woman struggling with a heavy load and be ready to help her, give her a hand. All this is necessary, and it is only when you have this sensitivity to everything that you can begin to work, to help and not reject or condemn.

Questioner: Pardon me, but you have not said who was your Master.

KRISHNAMURTI: Does it matter very much? Burn the book, thow it away. When you give importance to something so trivial as who the Master is, you are making the whole of existence into a very petty affair. You see, we always want to know who the Master is, who the learned person is, who the artist is that painted the picture. We never want to discover for ourselves the content of the picture irrespective of the identity of the artist. It is only when you know who the poet is that you say the poem is lovely. This is snobbishness, the mere repetition of an opinion, and it destroys your own inward perception of the reality of the thing. If you perceive that a picture is beautiful and you feel very grateful, does it really matter to you who painted it? If your one concern is to find the content, the truth of the picture, then the picture communicates its significance.

7
Ambition

We have been discussing how essential it is to have love, and we saw that one cannot acquire or buy it; yet without love, all our plans for a perfect social order in which there is no exploitation, no regimentation, will have no meaning at all, and I think it is very important to understand this while we are young.

Wherever one goes in the world, it does not matter where, one finds that society is in a perpetual state of conflict. There are always the powerful, the rich, the well-to-do on the one hand, and the labourers on the other; and each one is enviously competing, each one wants a higher position, a bigger salary, more power, greater prestige. That is the state of the world, and so there is always war going on both within and without.

Now, if you and I want to bring about a complete revolution in the social order, the first thing we have to understand is this instinct for the acquisition of power. Most of us want power in one form or another. We see that through wealth and power we shall be able to travel, associate with important people and become famous; or we dream of bringing about a perfect society. We think we shall achieve that which is good through power; but the very pursuit of power—power for ourselves, power for our country, power for an ideology—is evil, destructive, because it inevitably creates opposing powers, and so there is always conflict.

Is it not right, then, that education should help you, as you grow up, to perceive the importance of bringing about a world in which there is no conflict either within or without, a world in which you are not in confiict with your neighbour or with any group of people because the drive of ambition, which is the desire for position and power, has utterly ceased? And it is possible to create a society in which there will be no inward or outward conflict? Society is the relationship between you and me; and if our relationship is based on ambition, each one of us wanting to be more powerful than the other, then obviously we shall always be in conflict. So, can this cause of conflict be removed? Can we all educate ourselves not to be competitive, not to compare ourselves with somebody else, not to want this or that position—in a word, not to be ambitious at all?

When you go outside the school with your parents, when you read the newspapers or talk to people, you must have noticed that almost everybody wants to bring about a change in the world. And have you not also noticed that these very people are always in conflict with each other over something or other—over ideas, property, race, caste or religion? Your parents, your neighbours, the ministers and bureaucrats—are they not all ambitious, struggling for a better position, and therefore always in conflict with somebody? Surely, it is only when all this competitiveness is removed that there will be a peaceful society in which all of us can live happily, creatively.

Now, how is this to be done? Can regulation, legislation, or the training of your mind not to be ambitious, do away with ambition? Outwardly you may be trained not to be ambitious, socially you may cease to compete with others; but inwardly you will still be ambitious, will you not? And is it possible to sweep away completely this ambition, which is bringing so much misery to human beings? Probably you have not thought about it before, because nobody has talked to you like this; but now that somebody is talking to you about it, don't you want to find out if it is possible to live in this world richly, fully, happily, creatively, without the destructive drive of ambition, without competition? Don't you want to know how to live so that your life will not destroy another or cast a shadow across his path?

You see, we think this is a Utopian dream which can never be brought about in fact; but I am not talking about Utopia, that would be nonsense. Can you and I, who are simple, ordinary people, live creatively in this world without the drive of ambition which shows itself in various ways as the desire for power, position? You will find the right answer when you love what you are doing. If you are an engineer merely because you must earn a livelihood, or because your father or society expects it of you, that is another form of compulsion; and compulsion in any form creates a contradiction, conflict. Whereas, if you really love to be an engineer, or a scientist, or if you can plant a tree, or paint a picture, or write a poem, not to gain recognition but just because you love to do it, then you will find that you never compete with another. I think this is the real key: to love what you do.

But when you are young it is often very difficult to know what you love to do, because you want to do so many things. You want to be an engineer, a locomotive driver, an airplane pilot zooming along in the blue skies; or perhaps you want to be a famous orator or politician. You may want to be an artist, a chemist, a poet or a carpenter. You may want to work with your head, or do something with your hands. Is any of these things what you really love to do, or is your interest in them merely a reaction to social pressures? How can you find out? And is not the true purpose of education to *help* you to find out, so that as you grow up you can begin to give your whole mind, heart and body to that which you really love to do?

To find out what you love to do demands a great deal of intelligence; because, if you are afraid of not being able to earn a livelihood, or of not fitting into this rotten society, then you will never find out. But, if you are not frightened, if you refuse to be pushed into the groove of tradition by your parents, by your teachers, by the superficial demands of society, then there is a possibility of discovering what it is you really love to do. So, to discover, there must be no fear of not surviving.

But most of us are afraid of not surviving, we say, "What will happen to me if I don't do as my parents say, if I don't fit into this society?" Being frightened, we do as we are told, and in that there is no love, there is only contradiction; and this inner contradiction is one of the factors that bring about destructive ambition.

So, it is a basic function of education to help you to find out what you really love to do, so that you can give your whole mind and heart to it, because that creates human dignity, that sweeps away mediocrity, the petty bourgeois mentality. That is why it is very important to have the right teachers, the right atmosphere, so that you will grow up with the love which expresses itself in what you are doing. Without this love your examinations, your knowledge, your capacities, your position and possessions are just ashes, they have no meaning; without this love your actions are going to bring more wars, more hatred, more mischief and destruction.

All this may mean nothing to you, because outwardly you are still very young, but I hope it will mean something to your teachers—and also to you, somewhere inside.

Questioner: Why do you feel shy?

KRISHNAMURTI: You know, it is an extraordinary thing in life to be anonymous—not to be famous or great, not to be very learned, not to be a tremendous reformer or revolutionary, just to be nobody; and when one really feels that way, to be suddenly surrounded by a lot of curious people creates a sense of withdrawal. That is all.

Questioner: How can we realize truth in our daily life?

KRISHNAMURTI: You think that truth is one thing and your daily life is something else, and in your daily life you want to realize what you call truth. But is truth apart from daily life? When you grow up you will have to earn a livelihood, will you not? After all, that is what you are passing your examinations for: to prepare yourself to earn a livelihood. But many people don't care what field of work they enter as long as they are earning some money. As long as they get a job it does not matter to them if it means being a soldier, a policeman, a lawyer, or some kind of crooked business man.

Now, to find the truth of what constitutes a right means of livelihood is important, is it not? Because truth is in your life, not away from it. How you talk, what you say, how you smile, whether you are deceitful, playing up to people—all that is the truth in your daily life. So, before you become a soldier, a policeman, a lawyer or a sharp business man, must you not perceive the truth of these professions? Surely, unless you see the truth of what you do and are guided by that truth, your life becomes a hideous mess.

Let us look at the question of whether you should become a soldier, because the other professions are a little more complex. Apart from propaganda and what other people say, what is the truth concerning the profession of a soldier? If a man becomes a soldier it means that he must fight to protect his country, he must discipline his mind not to think but to obey. He must be prepared to kill or be killed—for what? For an idea that certain people, great or petty, have said is right. So you become a soldier in order to sacrifice yourself and to kill others. Is that a right profession? Don't ask somebody else, but find out for yourself the truth of the matter. You are told to kill for the sake of a marvellous Utopia in the future—as if the man who tells you knew all about the future! Do you think that killing is a right profession, whether it be for your country or for some organized religion? Is killing ever right at all?

So, if you want to discover the truth in that vital process which is your own life, you will have to inquire deeply into all these things; you will have to give your mind and heart to it. You will have to think independently, clearly, without prejudice for truth is not away from life, it is in the very movement of your daily living.

Questioner: Don't images, Masters and saints help us to meditate rightly?

KRISHNAMURTI: Do you know what right meditation is? Don't you want to discover for yourself the truth of the matter? And will you ever discover that truth if you accept on authority what right meditation is?

This is an immense question. To discover the art of meditation you must know the whole depth and breadth of this extraordinary process called thinking. If you accept some authority who says, "Meditate along these lines," you are merely a follower, the blind servant of a system or an idea. Your acceptance of authority is based on the hope of gaining a result, and that is not meditation.

Questioner: What are the duties of a student?

KRISHNAMURTI: What does the word 'duty' mean? Duty to what? Duty to your country according to a politician? Duty to your father and mother according to their wishes? They will say it is your duty to do as they tell you; and what they tell you is conditioned by their background, their tradition, and so on. And what is a student? Is it a boy or a girl who goes to school and reads a few books in order to pass some examination? Or is only he a student who is learning all the time and for whom there is therefore no end to learning? Surely, the person who merely reads up on a subject, passes an examination, and then drops it, is not a student. The real student is studying, learning, inquiring, exploring, not just until he is twenty or twenty-five, but throughout life.

To be a student is to learn all the time; and as long as you are learning, there is no teacher, is there? The moment you are a student there is no one in particular to teach you, because you are learning from everything. The leaf that is blown by the wind, the murmur of the waters on the banks of a river, the flight of a bird high in the air, the poor man as he walks by with a heavy load, the people who think they know everything about life—you are learning from them all, therefore there is no teacher and you are not a follower.

So the duty of a student is just to learn. There was once a famous painter in Spain whose name was Goya. He was one of the greatest, and when he was a very old man he wrote under one of his paintings, "I am still learning". You can learn from books, but that does not take you very far. A book can give you only what the author has to tell. But the learning that comes through self-knowledge has no limit, because to learn through your own self-knowledge is to know how to listen, how to observe, and therefore you learn from everything: from music, from what people say and the way they say it, from anger, greed, ambition.

This earth is *ours*, it does not belong to the communists, the socialists, or the capitalists; it is yours and mine, to be lived on happily, richly, without conflict. But that richness of life, that happiness, that feeling, "This earth is ours", cannot be brought about by enforcement, by law. It must come from within because we love the earth and all the things thereof; and that is the state of learning.

Questioner: What is the difference between respect and love?

KRISHNAMURTI: You can look up "respect" and "love" in a dictionary and find the answer. Is that what you want to know? Do you want to know the superficial meaning of those words, or the significance behind them?

When a prominent man comes around, a minister or a governor, have you noticed how everybody salutes him? You call that respect, don't you? But such respect is phony, because behind it there is fear, greed. You want something out of the poor devil, so you put a garland around his neck. That is not respect, it is merely the coin with which you buy and sell in the market. You don't feel respect for your servant or the villager, but only for those from whom you hope to get something. That kind of respect is really fear; it is not respect at all, it has no meaning. But if you really have love in your heart, then to you the governor, the teacher, your servant and the villager are all the same; then you have respect, a feeling for them all, because love does not ask anything in return.

8

Orderly Thinking

Among so many other things in life, have you ever considered why it is that most of us are rather sloppy—sloppy in our dress, in our manners, in our thoughts, in the way we do things? Why are we unpunctual and, so, inconsiderate of others? And what is it that brings about order in everything, order in our dress, in our thoughts, in our speech, in the way we walk, in the way we treat those who are less fortunate than ourselves? What brings about this curious order that comes without compulsion, without planning, without deliberate mentation? Have you ever considered it? Do you know what I mean by order? It is to sit quietly without pressure, to eat elegantly without rush, to be leisurely and yet precise, to be clear in one's thinking and yet expansive. What brings about this order in life? It is really a very important point, and I think that, if one could be educated to discover the factor that produces order, it would have great significance.

Surely, order comes into being only through virtue; for unless you are virtuous, not merely in the little things, but in all things, your life becomes chaotic, does it not? Being virtuous has very little meaning in itself; but because you are virtuous there is precision in your thought, order in your whole being, and that is the function of virtue.

But what happens when a man tries to *become* virtuous, when he disciplines himself to be kind, efficient, thoughtful, considerate, when he attempts not to hurt people, when he spends his energies in trying to establish order, in struggling to be good? His efforts only lead to respectability, which brings about mediocrity of mind; therefore he is not virtuous.

Have you ever looked very closely at a flower? How astonishingly precise it is, with all its petals; yet there is an extraordinary tenderness, a perfume, a loveliness about it. Now, when a man *tries* to be orderly, his life may be very precise, but it has lost that quality of gentleness which comes into being only when, like with the flower, there is no effort. So our difficulty is to be precise, clear and expansive without effort.

You see, the *effort* to be orderly or tidy has such a narrowing influence. If I deliberately try to be orderly in my room, if I am careful to put everything in its place, if I am always watching myself, where I put my feet, and so on, what happens? I become an intolerable bore to myself and to others. It is a tiresome person who is always trying to be something, whose thoughts are very carefully arranged, who chooses one thought in preference to another. Such a person may be very tidy, clear, he may use words precisely, he may be very attentive and considerate, but he has lost the creative joy of living.

So, what is the problem? How can one have this creative joy of living, be expansive in one's feeling, wide in one's thinking, and yet be precise, clear, orderly in one's life? I think most of us are not like that because we never feel anything intensely, we never give our hearts and minds to anything completely. I remember watching two red squirrels, with long bushy tails and lovely fur, chase each other up and down a tall tree for about ten minutes without stopping—just for the joy of living. But you and I cannot know that joy if we do not feel things deeply, if there is no passion in our lives—passion, not for doing good or bringing about some reform, but passion in the sense of feeling things very strongly; and we can have that vital passion only when there is a total revolution in our thinking, in our whole being.

Have you noticed how few of us have deep feeling about anything? Do you ever rebel against your teachers, against your parents, not just because you don't like something, but because you have a deep, ardent feeling that you don't want to do certain things? If you feel deeply and ardently about something, you will find that this very feeling in a curious way brings a new order into your life.

Orderliness, tidiness, clarity of thinking are not very important in themselves, but they become important to a man who is sensitive, who feels deeply, who is in a state of perpetual inward revolution. If you feel very strongly about the lot of the poor man, about the beggar who receives dust in his face as the rich man's car goes by, if you are extraordinarily receptive, sensitive to everything, then that very sensitivity brings orderliness, virtue; and I think this is very important for both the educator and the student to understand.

In this country, unfortunately, as all over the world, we care so little, we have no deep feeling about anything. Most of us are intellectuals—intellectuals in the superficial sense of being very clever, full of words and theories about what is right and what is wrong, about how we should think, what we should do. Mentally we are highly developed, but inwardly there is very little substance or significance; and it is this inward substance that brings about true action, which is not action according to an idea.

That is why you should have very strong feelings—

feelings of passion, anger—and watch them, play with them, find out the truth of them; for if you merely suppress them, if you say, "I must not get angry, I must not feel passionate, because it is wrong", you will find that your mind is gradually being encased in an idea and thereby becomes very shallow. You may be immensely clever, you may have encyclopaedic knowledge, but, if there is not the vitality of strong and deep feeling, your comprehension is like a flower that has no perfume.

It is very important for you to understand all these things while you are young, because then, when you grow up, you will be real revolutionaries—revolutionaries, not according to some ideology, theory or book, but revolutionaries in the total sense of the word, right through as integrated human beings, so that there is not a spot left in you which is contaminated by the old. Then your mind is fresh, innocent, and is therefore capable of extraordinary creativeness. But if you miss the significance of all this, your life will become very drab, for you will be overwhelmed by society, by your family, by your wife or husband, by theories, by religious or political organizations. That is why it is so urgent for you to be rightly educated—which means that you must have teachers who can help you to break through the crust of so-called civilization and be, not repetitive machines, but individuals who really have a song inside them and are therefore happy, creative human beings.

Questioner: What is anger and why does one get angry?

KRISHNAMURTI: If I tread on your toes, or pinch you, or take something away from you, won't you be angry? And why should you not be angry? Why do you think anger is wrong? Because somebody has told you? So, it is very important to find out why one is angry, to see the truth of anger, and not merely say it is wrong to be angry.

Now, why do you get angry? Because you don't want to be hurt—which is the normal human demand for survival. You feel that you should not be used, crushed, destroyed or exploited by an individual, a government or society. When somebody slaps you, you feel hurt, humiliated, and you don't like that feeling. If the person who hurts you is big and powerful so that you can't hit back, you in turn hurt somebody else, you take it out on your brother, your sister, or your servant if you have one. So the play of anger is kept going.

First of all, it is a natural response to avoid being hurt. Why should anybody exploit you? So, in order not to be hurt, you protect yourself, you begin to develop a defence, a barrier. Inwardly you build a wall around yourself by not being open, receptive; therefore you are incapable of exploration, of expansive feeling. You say anger is very bad and you condemn it, as you condemn various other feelings; so gradually you become arid, empty, you have no strong feelings at all. Do you understand?

Questioner: Why do we love our mothers so much?

KRISHNAMURTI: Do you love your mother if you hate your father? Listen carefully. When you love somebody very much, do you exclude others from that love? If you really love your mother, don't you also love your father, your aunt, your neighbour, your servant? Don't you have the feeling of love first, and then the love of someone in particular? When you say, "I love my mother very much", are you not being considerate of her? Can you then give her a lot of meaningless trouble? And if you are considerate of your mother, are you not also considerate of your brother, your sister, your neighbour? Otherwise you don't really love your mother; it is just a word, a convenience.

Questioner: I am full of hate. Will you please teach me how to love?

KRISHNAMURTI: No one can teach you how to love. If people could be taught how to love, the world problem would be very simple, would it not? If we could learn how to love from a book as we learn mathematics, this would be a marvellous world; there would be no hate, no exploitation, no wars, no division of rich and poor, and we would all be really friendly with each other. But love is not so easily come by. It is easy to hate, and hate brings people together after a fashion; it creates all kinds of fantasies, it brings about various types of cooperation as in war. But love is much more difficult. You cannot learn how to love, but what you can do is to observe hate and put it gently aside. Don't battle against hate, don't say how terrible it is to hate people, but see hate for what it is and let it drop away; brush it aside, it is not important. What is important is not to let hate take root in your mind. Do you understand? Your mind is like rich soil, and if given sufficient time any problem that comes along takes root like a weed, and then you have the trouble of pulling it out; but if you do not give the problem sufficient time to take root, then it has no place to grow and it will wither away. If you encourage hate, give it time to take root, to grow, to mature, it becomes an enormous problem. But if each time hate arises you let it go by, then you will find that your mind becomes very sensitive without being sentimental; therefore it will know love.

The mind can pursue sensations, desires, but it cannot

pursue love. Love must come to the mind. And, when once love is there, it has no division as sensuous and divine: it is love. That is the extraordinary thing about love: it is the only quality that brings a total comprehension of the whole of existence.

Questioner: What is happiness in life?

KRISHNAMURTI: If you want to do something pleasurable, you think you will be happy when you do it. You may want to marry the richest man, or the most beautiful girl, or pass some examination, or be praised by somebody, and you think that by getting what you want you will be happy. But is that happiness? Does it not soon fade away, like the flower that blossoms in the morning and withers in the evening? Yet that is our life, and that is all we want. We are satisfied with such superficialities: with having a car or a secure position, with feeling a little emotion over some futile thing, like boy who is happy flying a kite in a strong wind and a few minutes later is in tears. That is our life, and with that we are satisfied. We never say, "I will give my heart, my energy, my whole being to find out what happiness is". We are not very serious, we don't feel very strongly about it, so we are gratified with little things.

But happiness is not something that you can seek; it is a result, a by-product. If you pursue happiness for itself, it will have no meaning. Happiness comes uninvited; and the moment you are conscious that you are happy, you are no longer happy. I wonder if you have noticed this? When you are suddenly joyous about nothing in particular, there is just the freedom of smiling, of being happy; but, the moment you are conscious of it, you have lost it, have you not? Being self-consciously happy, or pursuing happiness, is the very ending of happiness. There is happiness only when the self and its demands are put aside.

You are taught a great deal about mathematics, you give your days to studying history, geography, science, physics, biology, and so on; but do you and your teachers spend any time at all thinking about these far more serious matters? Do you ever sit quietly, with your back very straight, without movement, and know the beauty of silence? Do you ever let your mind wander, not about petty things, but expansively, widely, deeply, and thereby explore, discover?

And do you know what is happening in the world? What is happening in the world is a projection of what is happening inside each one of us; what we are, the world is. Most of us are in turmoil, we are acquisitive, possessive, we are jealous and condemn people; and that is exactly what is happening in the world, only more dramatically, ruthlessly. But neither you nor your teachers spend any time thinking about all this; and it is only when you spend some time every day earnestly thinking about these matters that there is a possibility of bringing about a total revolution and creating a new world. And I assure you, a new world has to be created, a world which will not be a continuation of the same rotten society in a different form. But you cannot create a new world if your mind is not alert, watchful, expansively aware; and that is why it is so important, while you are young, to spend some time reflecting over these very serious matters and not just pass your days in the study of a few subjects, which leads nowhere except to a job and death. So do consider seriously all these things, for out of that consideration there comes an extraordinary feeling of joy, of happiness.

Questioner: What is real life?

KRISHNAMURTI: "What is real life?" A little boy has asked this question. Playing games, eating good food, running, jumping, pushing—that is real life for him. You see, we divide life into the real and the false. Real life is doing something which you love to do with your whole being so that there is no inner contradiction, no war between what you are doing and what you think you *should* do. Life is then a completely integrated process in which there is tremendous joy. But that can happen only when you are not psychologically depending on anybody, or on any society, when there is complete detachment inwardly, for only then is there a possibility of really loving what you do. If you are in a state of total revolution, it does not matter whether you garden, or become a prime minister, or do something else; you will love what you do, and out of that love there comes an extraordinary feeling of creativeness.

9

An Open Mind

You know, it is very interesting to find out what learning is. We learn from a book or from a teacher about mathematics, geography, history; we learn where London is, or Moscow, or New York; we learn how a machine works, or how the birds build their nests, care for their young, and so on. By observation and study we learn. That is one kind of learning.

But is there not also another kind of learning—the learning that comes through experience? When we see a boat on the river with its sails reflected on the quiet waters, is that not an extraordinary experience? And then what happens? The mind stores up an experience of that kind, just as it stores up knowledge, and the next evening we go out there to watch the boat, hoping to have the same kind of feeling—an experience of joy, that sense of peace which comes so rarely in our lives. So the mind is sedulously storing up experience; and it is this storing up of experience as memory that makes us think, is it not? What we call thinking is the response of memory. Having watched that boat on the river and felt a sense of joy, we store up the experience as memory and then want to repeat it; so the process of thinking is set going, is it not?

You see, very few of us really know how to think. Most of us merely repeat what we have read in a book, or what somebody has told us, or our thinking is the outcome of our own very limited experience. Even if we travel all over the world and have innumerable experiences, meet many different people and hear what they have to say, observe their customs, their religions, their manners, we retain the remembrance of all that, from which there is what we call thinking. We compare, judge, choose, and through this process we hope to find some reasonable attitude towards life. But that kind of thinking is very limited, it is confined to a very small area. We have an experience like seeing the boat on the river, or a corpse being carried to the *burning-ghats*, or a village woman carrying a heavy burden—all these impressions are there, but we are so insensitive that they don't sink into us and ripen; and it is only through sensitivity to everything around us that there is the beginning of a different kind of thinking which is not limited by our conditioning.

If you hold firmly to some set of beliefs or other, you look at everything through that particular prejudice or tradition; you don't have any contact with reality. Have you ever noticed the village women carrying heavy burdens to the town? When you do notice it, what happens to you, what do you feel? Or is it that you have seen these women going by so often that you have no feeling at all because you have become used to it and, so, hardly notice them? And even when you observe something for the first time, what happens? You automatically translate what you see according to your prejudices, don't you? You experience it according to your conditioning as a communist, a socialist, a capitalist, or some other "ist." Whereas, if you are none of these things and therefore do not look through the screen of any idea or belief, but actually have the direct contact, then you will notice what an extraordinary relationship there is between you and what you observe. If you have no prejudice, no bias, if you are open, then everything around you becomes extraordinarily interesting, tremendously alive.

That is why it is very important, while you are young, to notice all these things. Be aware of the boat on the river, watch the train go by, see the peasant carrying a heavy burden, observe the insolence of the rich, the pride of the ministers, of the big people, of those who think they know a lot—just watch them, don't criticize. The moment you criticize, you are not in relationship, you already have a barrier between yourself and them; but if you merely observe, then you will have a direct relationship with people and with things. If you can observe alertly, keenly, but without judging, without concluding, you will find that your thinking becomes astonishingly acute. Then you are learning all the time.

Everywhere around you there is birth and death, the struggle for money, position, power, the unending process of what we call life; and don't you sometimes wonder, even while you are very young, what it is all about? You see, most of us want an answer, we want to be *told* what it is all about, so we pick up a political or religious book, or we ask somebody to tell us; but no one can tell us, because life is not something which can be understood from a book, nor can its significance be gathered by following another, or through some form of prayer. You and I must understand it for ourselves—which we can do only when we are fully alive, very alert, watchful, observant, taking interest in everything around us; and then we shall discover what it is to be really happy.

Most people are unhappy; and they are unhappy because there is no love in their hearts. Love will arise in your heart when you have no barrier between yourself and another, when you meet and observe people without judging them, when you just see the sailboat on the river and enjoy the beauty of it. Don't let your prejudices cloud your observation of things as they are; just observe, and you will discover that out of this simple observation, out of this awareness of trees, of birds, of people walking, working, smiling, something happens to you inside. Without this extraordinary thing happening to you, without the arising of love in your heart, life has very little meaning; and that is why it is so important that the educator should be educated to help you understand the significance of all these things.

Questioner: Why do we want to live in luxury?

KRISHNAMURTI: What do you mean by luxury? Having clean clothes, keeping your body clean, eating good food—do you call that luxury? It may seem to be luxury to the man who is starving, clothed in rags, and who can't take a bath every day. So luxury varies according to one's desires; it is a matter of degree.

Now, do you know what happens to you if you are fond of luxury, if you are attached to comfort and always want to sit on a sofa or in an overstuffed chair? Your mind goes to sleep. It is good to have a little bodily comfort; but to emphasize comfort, to give it great importance, is to have a sleepy mind. Have you noticed how happy most fat people are? Nothing seems to disturb them through their many layers of fat. That is a physical condition, but the mind also puts on layers of fat; it does not want to be questioned or otherwise disturbed, and such a mind gradually goes to sleep. What we now call education generally puts the student to sleep, because if he asks really sharp, penetrating questions, the teacher gets very disturbed and says, "Let us get on with our lesson."

So, when the mind is attached to any form of comfort, when it is attached to a habit, to a belief, or to a particular spot which it calls "my home," it begins to go to sleep; and to understand this fact is more important than to ask whether or not we live luxuriously. The mind which is very active, alert, watchful, is never attached to comfort; luxury means nothing to it. But merely having very few clothes does not mean that one has an alert mind. The *sannyasi* who outwardly lives very simply may be inwardly very complex, cultivating virtue, wanting to attain truth, God. What is important is to be inwardly very simple, very austere, which is to have a mind not clogged with beliefs, with fears, with innumerable wants, for only such a mind is capable of real thinking, of exploration and discovery.

Questioner: Can there be peace in our life as long as we are struggling with our environment?

KRISHNAMURTI: Must you not struggle with your environment? Must you not break through it? What your parents believe, your social background, your traditions, the kind of food you eat, and the things around you like religion, the priest, the rich man, the poor man—all that is your environment. And must you not break through that environment by questioning it, by being in revolt against it? If you are not in revolt, if you merely accept your environment, there is a kind of peace, but it is the peace of death; whereas, if you struggle to break through the environment and find out for yourself what is true, then you will discover a different kind of peace which is not mere stagnation. It is essential to struggle with your environment. You must. Therefore peace is not important. What is important is to understand and break through your environment; and from that comes peace. But, if you seek peace by merely accepting your environment, you will be put to sleep, and then you may as well die. That is why from the tenderest age there should be in you a sense of revolt. Otherwise you will just decay, won't you?

Questioner: Are you happy or not?

KRISHNAMURTI: I don't know. I have never thought about it. The moment you think you are happy, you cease to be happy, don't you? When you are playing and shouting with joy, what happens the moment you become conscious that you are joyous? You stop being joyous. Have you noticed it? So happiness is something which is not within the field of self-consciousness.

When you try to be good, are you good? Can goodness be practised? Or is goodness something that comes naturally because you see, observe, understand? Similarly, when you are conscious that you are happy, happiness goes out of the window. To seek happiness is absurd, because there is happiness only when you don't seek it.

Do you know what the word "humility" means? And can you cultivate humility? If you repeat every morning, "I am going to be humble," is that humility? Or does humility arise of itself when you no longer have pride, vanity? In the same way, when the things that prevent happiness are gone, when anxiety, frustration, the search for one's own security have ceased, then happiness is there, you don't have to seek it.

Why are most of you so silent? Why don't you discuss with me? You know, it is important to express your thoughts and feelings, however badly, because it will mean a great deal to you, and I will tell you why. If you begin to express your thoughts and feelings now, however hesitantly, as you grow up you will not be smothered by your environment, by your parents, by society, tradition. But unfortunately your teachers don't encourage you to question, they don't ask you what you think.

Questioner: Why do we cry, and what is sorrow?

KRISHNAMURTI: A little boy wants to know why we cry and what is sorrow. When do you cry? You cry when somebody takes away your toy, or when you get hurt, or when you don't win a game, or when your teacher or your parents scold you, or when somebody hits you. As you grow older you cry less and less, because you harden yourself against life. Very few of us cry when we are older because we have lost the extraordinary sensitivity of childhood. But sorrow is not merely the loss of something, it is not just the feeling of being stopped, frustrated; sorrow is something much deeper. You see, there is such a thing as having no understanding. If there is no understanding, there is great sorrow. If the mind does not penetrate beyond its own barriers, there is misery.

Questioner: How can we become integrated without conflict?

KRISHNAMURTI: Why do you object to conflict? You all seem to think conflict is a dreadful thing. At present you and I are in conflict, are we not? I am trying to tell you something, and you don't understand; so there is a sense of friction, conflict. And what is wrong with friction, conflict, disturbance? Must you not be disturbed? Integration does not come when you seek it by avoiding conflict. It is only through conflict, and the understanding of conflict, that there is integration.

Integration is one of the most difficult things to come by, because it means a complete unification of your whole being in all that you do, in all that you say, in all that you think. You cannot have integration without understanding relationship—your relationship with society, your relationship with the poor man, the villager, the beggar, with the millionaire and the governor. To understand relationship you must struggle with it, you must question and not merely accept the values established by tradition, by your parents, by the priest, by the religion and the economic system of the society about you. That is why it is essential for you to be in revolt, otherwise you will never have integration.

10

Inward Beauty

I am sure we all have sometime or other experienced a great sense of tranquillity and beauty coming to us from the green fields, the setting sun, the still waters, or the snow-capped peaks. But what is beauty? Is it merely the appreciation that we feel, or is beauty a thing apart from perception? If you have good taste in clothes, if you use colours thtat harmonize, if you have dignified manners, if you speak quietly and hold yourself erect, all that makes for beauty, does it not? But that is merely the outward expression of an inward state, like a poem you write or a picture you paint. You can look at the green field reflected in the river and experience no sense of beauty, just pass it by. If, like the fisherman, you see every day the swallows flying low over the water, it probably means very little to you; but if you are aware of the extraordinary beauty of something like that, what is it that happens within you and makes you say, "How very beautiful?" What goes to make up this inward sense of beauty? There is the beauty of outward form: tasteful clothes, nice pictures, attractive furniture, or no furniture at all with bare, well-proportioned walls, windows that are perfect in shape, and so on. I am not talking merely of that, but of what goes to make up this inward beauty.

Surely, to have this inward beauty, there must be

complete abandonment; the sense of not being held, of no restraint, no defence, no resistence; but abandonment becomes chaotic if there is no austerity with it. And do we know what it means to be austere, to be satisfied with little and not to think in terms of "the more"? There must be this abandonment with deep inward austerity—the austerity that is extraordinarily simple because the mind is not acquiring, gaining, not thinking in terms of "the more". It is the simplicity born of abandonment with austerity that brings about the state of creative beauty. But if there is no love you cannot be simple, you cannot be austere. You may talk about simplicity and austerity, but without love they are merely a form of compulsion, and therefore there is no abandonment. Only he has love who abandons himself, forgets himself completely, and thereby brings about the state of creative beauty.

Beauty obviously includes beauty of form; but without inward beauty, the mere sensual appreciation of beauty of form leads to degradation, disintegration. There is inward beauty only when you feel real love for people and for all the things of the earth; and with that love there comes a tremendous sense of consideration, watchfulness, patience. You may have perfect technique, as a singer or a poet, you may know how to paint or put words together, but without this creative beauty inside, your talent will have very little significance.

Unfortunately, most of us are becoming mere technicians. We pass examinations, acquire this or that technique in order to earn a livelihood; but to acquire technique or develop capacity without paying attention to the inner state, brings about ugliness and chaos in the world. If we awaken creative beauty inwardly, it expresses itself outwardly, and then there is order. But that is much more difficult than acquiring a technique, because it means abandoning ourselves completely, being without fear, without restraint, without resistance, without defence; and we can thus abandon ourselves only when there is austerity, a sense of great inward simplicity. Outwardly we may be simple, we may have but few clothes and be satisfied with one meal a day; but that is not austerity. There is austerity when the mind is capable of infinite experience—when it has experience, and yet remains very simple. But that state can come into being only when the mind is no longer thinking in terms of 'the more', in terms of having or becoming something through time.

What I am talking about may be difficult for you to understand, but it is really quite important. You see, technicians are not creators; and there are more and more technicians in the world, people who know what to do and how to do it, but who are not creators. In America there are calculating machines capable of solving in a few minutes mathematical problems which would take a man, working ten hours every day, a hundred years to solve. These extraordinary machines are being developed. But machines can never be creators—and human beings are becoming more and more like machines. Even when they rebel, their rebellion is within the limits of the machine and is therefore no rebellion at all.

So it is very important to find out what it is to be creative. You can be creative only when there is abandonment—which means, really, when there is no sense of compulsion, no fear of not being, of not gaining, of not arriving. Then there is great austerity, simplicity, and with it there is love. The whole of that is beauty, the state of creativeness.

Questioner: Does the soul survive after death?

KRISHNAMURTI: If you really want to know, how are you going to find out? By reading what Shankara, Buddha or Christ has said about it? By listening to your own particular leader or saint? They may all be totally wrong. Are you prepared to admit this—which means that your mind is in a position to inquire?

You must first find out, surely, whether there is a soul to survive. What is the soul? Do you know what it is? Or have you merely been told that there is a soul—told by your parents, by the priest, by a particular book, by your cultural environment—and accepted it?

The word "soul" implies something beyond mere physical existence, does it not? There is your physical body, and also your character, your tendencies, your virtues; and transcending all this you say there is the soul. If that state exists at all, it must be spiritual, something which has the quality of timelessness; and you are asking whether that spiritual something survives death. That is one part of the question.

The other part is: what is death? Do you know what death is? You want to know if there is survival after death; but, you see, that question is not important. The important question is: can you know death while you are living? What significance has it if someone tells you that there is or is not survival after death? You still do not know. But you can find out for yourself what death is, not after you are dead, but while you are living, healthy, vigorous, while you are thinking, feeling.

This is also part of education. To be educated is not only to be proficient in mathematics, history or geography, it is also to have the ability to understand this extraordinary thing called death—not when you are physically dying, but while you are living, while you are laughing, while you are climbing a tree, while you are sailing a boat or swimming. Death is the unknown, and what matters is to know of the unknown while you are living.

Questioner: When we become ill, why do our parents worry and worry about us?

KRISHNAMURTI: Most parents are at least partly concerned to look after their children, care for them, but when they worry and worry it indicates that they are more concerned about themselves than about their children. They don't want you to die, because they say, "If our son or daughter dies, what is going to become of us?" If parents loved their children, do you know what would happen? If your parents really loved you, they would see to it that you had no cause for fear, that you were healthy and happy human beings; they would see to it that there was no war, no poverty in the world, that society did not destroy you or anyone around you, whether the villagers, or the people in the towns, or the animals. It is because parents do not truly love their children that there are wars, that there are the rich and the poor. They have invested their own beings in their children and through their children they hope to continue, and if you become seriously ill they worry; so they are concerned with their own sorrow. But they will not admit that.

You see, property, land, name, wealth and family are the means of one's own continuity, which is also called immortality; and when something happens to their children, parents are horrified, driven to great sorrow, because they are primarily concerned about themselves. If parents were really concerned about their children, society would be transformed overnight; we would have a different kind of education, different homes, a world without war.

Questioner: Should the temples be open to all for worship?

KRISHNAMURTI: What is the temple? It is a place of worship in which there is a symbol of God, the symbol being an image conceived by the mind and carved out of stone by the hand. That stone, that image, is not God, is it? It is only a symbol, and a symbol is like your shadow as you walk in the sun. The shadow is not you; and these images, these symbols in the temple, are not God, not truth. So what does it matter who enters or who does not enter the temple? Why make such a fuss about it? Truth may be under a dead leaf, it may be in a stone by the wayside, in the waters that reflect the loveliness of an evening, in the clouds, in the smile of the woman who carries a burden. In this whole world there is reality, not necessarily in the temple; and generally it is *not* in the temple, because that temple is made out of man's fear, it is based on his desire for security, on his divisions of creed and caste. This world is ours, we are human beings living together, and if a man is seeking God he shuns temples because they divide people. The Christian church, the Mohammedan mosque, your own Hindu temple—they all divide people, and a man who is seeking God will have none of these things. So the question of whether or not someone or other should enter the temple becomes merely a political issue; it has no reality.

Questioner: What part does discipline play in our lives?

KRISHNAMURTI: Unfortunately it plays a great part, does it not? A great part of your life is disciplined: do *this* and don't do *that*. You are told when to get up, what to eat and what not to eat, what you must know and not know; you are told that you must read, go to classes, pass examinations, and so on. Your parents, your teachers, your society, your tradition, your sacred books all tell you what to do; so your life is bound, hedged about by discipline, is it not? You are a prisoner of *do's* and *don'ts*, they are the bars of your cage.

Now, what happens to a mind that is bound by discipline? Surely, it is only when you are afraid of something, when you are resisting something, that there has to be discipline; then you have to control, hold yourself together. Either you do this out of your own volition, or society does it for you—society being your parents, your teachers, your tradition, your sacred books. But if you begin to inquire, to search out, if you learn and understand without fear, then is discipline necessary? Then that very understanding brings about its own true order, which is not born of imposition or compulsion.

Do think about this; because when you are disciplined through fear, crushed by the compulsion of society, dominated by what your parents and teachers say, there is for you no freedom, no joy, and all initiative is gone. The older the culture, the greater is the weight of tradition which disciplines you, tells you what you must and must not do; and so you are weighed down, psychologically flattened as if a steam-roller had gone over you. That is what has happened in India. The weight of tradition is so enormous that all initiative has been destroyed, and you have ceased to be an individual; you are merely part of a social machine, and with that you are content. Do you understand? You don't revolt, explode, break away. Your parents don't want you to revolt, your teachers don't want you to break away, therefore your education is aimed at making you conform to the established pattern. Then you are not a complete human being, because fear gnaws at your heart; and as long as there is fear there is no joy, no creativity.

Questioner: Just now, when you were talking about the temple, you referred to the symbol of God as merely a shadow. We cannot see the shadow of a man without the real man to cast it.

KRISHNAMURTI: Are you satisfied with the shadow? If you are hungry, will you be satisfied merely to look at food? Then why be satisfied with the shadow in the temple? If you deeply want to understand the real, you will let the shadow go. But, you see, you are mesmerized by the shadow, by the symbol, by the image of stone. Look what has happened in the world. People are divided because they worship a particular shadow in the mosque, in the temple, in the church. There can be the multiplication of shadows, but there is only one reality, which cannot be divided; and to reality there is no path, neither Christian, Moslem, Hindu, nor any other.

Questioner: Examinations may be unnecessary for the rich boy or girl whose future is assured, but are they not a necessity for poor students who must be prepared to earn a livelihood? And is their need less urgent, especially if we take society as it is?

KRISHNAMURTI: You take society as it is for granted. Why? You who don't belong to the poor class, who are fairly well-to-do, why don't you revolt—not as a communist or a socialist, but revolt against the whole social system? You can afford to do it, so why don't you use your intelligence to find out what is true and create a new society? The poor man is not going to revolt, because he hasn't the energy or the time to think; he is wholly occupied, he wants food, work. But you who have leisure, a little free time to use your intelligence, why don't *you* revolt? Why don't you find out what is a right society, a true society, and build a new civilization? If it does not begin with you, it will obviously not begin with the poor.

Questioner: Will the rich ever be prepared to give up much of what they have for the sake of the poor?

KRISHNAMURTI: We are not talking about what the rich should give up for the sake of the poor. Whatever they give up, it will still not satisfy the poor—but that is not the problem. You who are well-to-do, and who therefore have the opportunity to cultivate intelligence, can you not through revolt create a new society? It depends on you, not on anybody else; it depends on each one of us, not on the rich or the poor, or on the communists. You see, most of us have not this spirit of revolt, this urge to break through, to find out; and it is this spirit that is important.

II

Conformity and Revolt

Have you ever sat very quietly with closed eyes and watched the movement of your own thinking? Have you watched your mind working—or rather, has your mind watched itself in operation, just to see what your thoughts are, what your feelings are, how you look at the trees, at the flowers, at the birds, at people, how you respond to a suggestion or react to a new idea? Have you ever done this? If you have not, you are missing a great deal. To know how one's mind works is a basic purpose of education. If you don't know how your mind reacts, if your mind is not aware of its own activities, you will never find out what society is. You may read books on sociology, study social sciences, but if you don't know how your own mind works you cannot actually understand what society is, because your mind is part of society; it *is* society. Your reactions, your beliefs, your going to the temple, the clothes you wear, the things you do and don't do and what you think—society is made up of all this, it is the replica of what is going on in your own mind. So your mind is not apart from society, it is not distinct from your culture, from your religion, from your various class divisions, from the ambitions and conflicts of the many. All this is society, and you are part of it. There is no "you" separate from society.

Now, society is always trying to control, to shape, to mould the thinking of the young. From the moment you are born and begin to receive impressions, your father and mother are constantly telling you what to do and what not to do, what to believe and what not to believe; you are told that there is God, or that there is no God but the State and that some dictator is its prophet. From childhood these things are poured into you, which means that your mind—which is very young, impressionable, inquisitive, curious to know, wanting to find out—is gradually being encased, conditioned, shaped so that you will fit into the pattern of a particular society and not be a revolutionary. Since the habit of patterned thinking has already been established in you, even if you do "revolt" it is within the pattern. It is like prisoners revolting in order to have better food, more conveniences—but always within the prison. When you seek God, or try to find out what is right government, it is always within the pattern of society, which says, "This is true and that is false, this is good and that is bad, this is the right leader and these are the saints." So your revolt, like the so-called revolution brought about by ambitious or very clever people, is always limited by the past. That is not revolt, that is not revolution: it is merely heightened activity, a more valiant struggle within the pattern. Real revolt, true revolution is to break away from the pattern and to inquire outside of it.

You see, all reformers—it does not matter *who* they are—are merely concerned with bettering the conditions within the prison. They never tell you not to conform, they never say, "Break through the walls of tradition and authority, shake off the conditioning that holds the mind." And that is real education: not merely to require you to pass examinations for which you have crammed up, or to write out something which you have learnt by heart, but to help you to see the walls of this prison in which the mind is held. Society influences all of us, it constantly shapes our thinking, and this pressure of society from the outside is gradually translated as the inner; but, however deeply it penetrates, it is still from the outside, and there is no such thing as the inner as long as you do not break through this conditioning. You must know what you are thinking, and whether you are thinking as a Hindu, or a Moslem, or a Christian; that is, in terms of the religion you happen to belong to. You must be conscious of what you believe or do not believe. All this is the pattern of society and, unless you are aware of the pattern and break away from it, you are still a prisoner though you may think you are free.

But you see, most of us are concerned with revolt within the prison; we want better food, a little more light, a larger window so that we can see a little more of the sky. We are concerned with whether the outcaste should enter the temple or not; we want to break down this particular caste, and in the very breaking down of one caste we create another, a "superior" caste; so we remain prisoners, and there is no freedom in prison. Freedom lies outside the walls, outside the pattern of society; but to be free of that pattern you have to understand the whole content of it, which is to understand your own mind. It is the mind that has created the present civilization, this tradition-bound culture or society and, without understanding your own mind, merely to revolt as a communist, a socialist, this or that, has very little meaning. That is why it is very important to have self-knowledge, to be aware of all your activities, your thoughts and feelings; and this is education, is it not? Because when you are fully aware of yourself your mind becomes very sensitive, very alert.

You try this—not someday in the far-away future, but

tomorrow or this afternoon. If there are too many people in your room, if your home is crowded, then go away by yourself, sit under a tree or on the river bank and quietly observe how your mind works. Don't correct it, don't say, "This is right, that is wrong", but just watch it as you would a film. When you go to the cinema you are not taking part in the film; the actors and actresses are taking part, but you are only watching. In the same way, watch how your mind works. It is really very interesting, far more interesting than any film, because your mind is the residue of the whole world and it contains all that human beings have experienced. Do you understand? Your mind is humanity, and when you perceive this, you will have immense compassion. Out of this understanding comes great love; and then you will know, when you see lovely things, what beauty is.

Questioner: How did you learn all that you are talking about, and how can we come to know it?

KRISHNAMURTI: That is a good question, is it not?

Now, if I may talk about myself a little, I have not read any books about these things, neither the *Upanishads*, the *Bhagavad Gita*, nor any psychological books; but as I told you, if you watch your own mind, it is all there. So when once you set out on the journey of self-knowledge, books are not important. It is like entering a strange land where you begin to find out new things and make astonishing discoveries; but, you see, that is all destroyed if you give importance to yourself. The moment you say, "I have discovered, I know, I am a great man because I have found out this and that," you are lost. If you have to take a long journey, you must carry very little; if you want to climb to a great height, you must travel light.

So this question is really important, because discovery and understanding come through self-knowledge, through observing the ways of the mind. What you say of your neighbour, how you talk, how you walk, how you look at the skies, at the birds, how you treat people, how you cut a branch—all these things are important, because they act like mirrors that show you as you are and, if you are alert, you discover everything anew from moment to moment.

Questioner: Should we form an idea about someone, or not?

KRISHNAMURTI: Should you have ideas about people? Should you form an opinion, make a judgment about someone? When you have ideas about your teacher, what is important to you? Not your teacher, but your ideas about him. And that is what happens in life, is it not? We all have opinions about people; we say, "He is good," "He is vain," "He is superstitious," "He does this or that." We have a screen of ideas between ourselves and another person, so we never really meet that person. Having seen someone do something, we say, "He has done this thing"; so it become important to date events. Do you understand? If you see someone do something which you consider to be good or bad, you then have an opinion of him which tends to become fixed and, when you meet that person ten days or a year later, you still think of him in terms of your opinion. But during this period he may have changed; therefore it is very important not to say, "He is like that," but to say, "He was like that in February," because by the end of the year he may be entirely different. If you say of anyone, "I know that person," you may be totally wrong, because you know him only up to a certain point, or by the events which took place on a particular date, and beyond that you don't know him at all. So what is important is to meet another human being always with a fresh mind, and not with your prejudices, with your fixed ideas, with your opinions.

Questioner: What is feeling and how do we feel?

KRISHNAMURTI: If you have lessons in physiology, your teacher has probably explained to you how the whole human nervous system is built up. When somebody pinches you, you feel pain. What does that mean? Your nerves carry a sensation to the brain, the brain translates it as pain, and then you say, "You have hurt me." Now, that is the physical part of feeling.

Similarly, there is psychological feeling, is there not? If you think you are marvellously beautiful and somebody says, "You are an ugly person," you feel hurt. Which means what? You hear certain words which the brain translates as unpleasant or insulting, and you are disturbed; or somebody flatters you, and you say, "How pleasurable it is to hear this." So feeling-thinking is a reaction—a reaction to a pin-prick, to an insult, to flattery, and so on. The whole of this is the process of feeling-thinking; but it is much more complex than this, and you can go deeper and deeper into it.

You see, when we have a feeling, we always name it, don't we? We say it is pleasurable or painful. When we are angry we give that feeling a name, we call it anger; but have you ever thought what would happen if you did not name a feeling? You try it. The next time you get angry, don't name it, don't call it anger; just be aware of the feeling without giving it a name, and see what happens.

Questioner: What is the difference between Indian culture and American culture?

KRISHNAMURTI: When we talk about American culture we generally mean the European culture which was transplanted in America, a culture which has since become modified and extended in meeting new frontiers, physical as well as mental.

And what is Indian culture? What is the culture which you have here? What do you mean by the word "culture"? If you have ever done any gardening you know how you cultivate and prepare the soil. You dig, remove rocks, and if necessary you add compost, a decomposed mixture of leaves, hay, manure, and other kinds of organic matter, to make the soil rich, and then you plant. The rich soil gives nourishment to the plant, and the plant gradually produces that marvellously lovely thing called a rose.

Now, the Indian culture is like that. Millions of people have produced it by their struggles, by exercising their will, by wanting this and resisting that, constantly thinking, suffering, fearing, avoiding, enjoying; also climate, food and clothing have had their influence on it. So we have here an extraordinary soil, the soil being the mind; and before it was completely moulded, there were a few vital, creative people who exploded all over Asia. They did not say, as you do, "I must accept the edicts of society. What will my father think if I do not?" On the contrary, they were people who had found something and they were not lukewarm, they were hot about it. Now, the whole of that is the Indian culture. What you think, the food you eat, the clothes you put on, your manners, your traditions, your speech, your paintings and statues, your gods, your priests and your sacred books—all that is the Indian culture, is it not?

So the Indian culture is somewhat different from the European culture, but underneath the movement is the same. This movement may express itself differently in America, because the demands are different there; there is less tradition and they have more refrigerators, cars, and so on. But it is the same movement underneath—the movement to find happiness, to find out what God, what truth is; and when this movement stops, culture declines, as it has done in this country. When this movement is blocked by authority, by tradition, by fear, there is decay, deterioration.

The urge to find out what truth is, what God is, is the only real urge and all other urges are subsidiary. When you throw a stone into still water, it makes expanding circles. The expanding circles are the subsidiary movements, the social reactions, but the real movement is at the centre, which is the movement to find happiness, God, truth; and you cannot find it as long as you are caught in fear, held by a threat. From the moment there is the arising of threat and fear, culture declines.

That is why it is very important, while you are young, *not* to become conditioned, *not* to be held in by fear of your parents, of society, so that there is in you this timeless movement to discover what is truth. The men who seek out what is truth, what is God—only such men can create a new civilization, a new culture; not the people who conform, or who merely revolt within the prison of the old conditioning. You may put on the robes of an ascetic, join this society or that, leave one religion for another, try in various ways to be free; but unless there is within you this movement to find out what is the real, what is truth, what is love, your efforts will be without significance. You may be very learned and do the things which society calls good, but they are all within the prison-walls of tradition and therefore of no revolutionary value at all.

Questioner: What do you think of Indians?

KRISHNAMURTI: That is really an innocent question, is it not? To see facts without opinion is one thing, but to have opinions about facts is totally another. It is one thing just to see the fact that a whole people are caught in superstition, in fear, but quite another to see that fact and condemn it. Opinions are not important, because I will have one opinion, you will have another, and a third person will have still another. To be concerned with opinions is a stupid form of thinking. What is important is to see facts as they are without opinion, without judging, without comparing.

To feel beauty without opinion is the only real perception of beauty. Similarly, if you can see the people of India just as they are, see them very clearly without fixed opinions, without judging, then what you see will be the real.

The Indians have certain manners, certain customs of their own, but fundamentally they are like any other people. They get bored, they are cruel, they are afraid, they revolt within the prison of society, just as people do everywhere else. Like the Americans, they also want comfort, only at present they do not have it to the same extent. They have a heavy tradition about renouncing the world and trying to be saintly; but they also have deep-rooted ambitions, hypocrisy, greed, envy, and they are broken up by castes, as human beings are everywhere else, only here it is much more brutal. Here in India you can see more closely the whole phenomenon of what is happening in the world. We want to be loved, but we don't know what love is; we are unhappy, thirsting for something real, and we turn to books, to the *Upanishads*, the *Gita*, or the Bible, so we get lost in words, in speculations. Whether it is here, or in Russia, or in America, the human mind is similar, only it expresses itself in different ways under different skies and different governments.

12

The Confidence of Innocence

We have been discussing the question of revolt within the prison: how all reformers, idealists, and others who are incessantly active in producing certain results, are always revolting within the walls of their own conditioning, within the walls of their own social structure, within the cultural pattern of civilization which is an expression of the collective will of the many. I think it would now be worth while if we could see what confidence is and how it comes about.

Through initiative there comes about confidence; but initiative within the pattern only brings *self*-confidence, which is entirely different from confidence without the self. Do you know what it means to have confidence? If you do something with your own hands, if you plant a tree and see it grow, if you paint a picture, or write a poem, or, when you are older, build a bridge or run some administrative job extremely well, it gives you confidence that you are able to do something. But, you see, confidence as we know it now is always within the prison, the prison which society—whether communist, Hindu, or Christian—has built around us. Initiative within the prison does create a certain confidence, because you feel you can do things: you can design a motor, be a very good doctor, an excellent scientist, and so on. But this feeling of confidence which comes with the capacity to succeed within the social structure, or to reform, to give more light, to decorate the interior of the prison is really *self*-confidence; you know you can do something, and you feel important in doing it. Whereas, when through investigating, through understanding, you break away from the social structure of which you are a part, there comes an entirely different kind of confidence which is without the sense of self-importance; and if we can understand the difference between these two—between self-confidence, and confidence without the self—I think it will have great significance in our life.

When you play a game very well, like badminton, cricket, or football, you have a certain sense of confidence, have you not? It gives you the feeling that you are pretty good at it. If you are quick at solving mathematical problems, that also breeds a sense of self-assurance. When confidence is born of action within the social structure, there always goes with it a strange arrogance, does there not? The confidence of a man who can do things, who is capable of achieving results, is always coloured by this arrogance of the self, the feeling, "It is I who do it". So, in the very act of achieving a result, of bringing about a social reform within the prison, there is the arrogance of the self, the feeling that *I* have done it, that *my* ideal is important, that *my* group has succeeded. This sense of the "me" and the "mine" always goes with the confidence that expresses itself within the social prison.

Have you not noticed how arrogant idealists are? The political leaders who bring about certain results, who achieve great reforms—have you not noticed that they are full of themselves, puffed up with their ideals and their achievements? In their own estimation they are very important. Read a few of the political speeches, watch some of these people who call themselves reformers, and you will see that in the very process of reformation they are cultivating their own ego; their reforms, however extensive, are still within the prison, therefore they are destructive and ultimately bring more misery and conflict to man.

Now, if you can see through this whole social structure, the cultural pattern of the collective will which we call civilization—if you can understand all that and break away from it, break through the prison walls of your particular society, whether Hindu, communist, or Christian, then you will find that there comes a confidence which is not tainted with the sense of arrogance. It is the confidence of innocence. It is like the confidence of a child who is so completely innocent he will try anything. It is this innocent confidence that will bring about a new civilization; but this innocent confidence cannot come into being as long as you remain within the social pattern.

Please do listen to this carefully. The speaker is not in the least important, but it is very important for you to understand the truth of what is being said. After all, that is education, is it not? The function of education is not to make you fit into the social pattern; on the contrary, it is to help you to understand completely, deeply, fully and thereby break away from the social pattern, so that you are an individual without that arrogance of the self; but you have confidence because you are really innocent.

Is it not a great tragedy that almost all of us are only concerned either with how to fit into society, or how to reform it? Have you noticed that most of the questions you have asked reflect this attitude? You are saying, in effect, "How can I fit into society? What will my father and mother say, and what will happen to me if I don't?" Such an attitude destroys whatever confidence, whatever initiative you have. And you leave school and college like so many automatons, highly efficient perhaps, but without any creative flame. That is why it is so important to understand the society, the environment in which one lives, and, in that very process of understanding, break away from it.

You see, this is a problem all over the world. Man is seeking a new response, a new approach to life, because the old ways are decaying, whether in Europe, in Russia, or here. Life is a continual challenge, and merely to try to bring about a better economic order is not a total response to that challenge, which is always new; and when cultures, peoples, civilizations are incapable of responding totally to the challenge of the new, they are destroyed.

Unless you are properly educated, unless you have this extraordinary confidence of innocence, you are inevitably going to be absorbed by the collective and lost in mediocrity. You will put some letters after your name, you will be married, have children, and that will be the end of you.

You see, most of us are frightened. Your parents are frightened, your educators are frightened, the governments and religions are frightened of your becoming a total individual, because they all want you to remain safely within the prison of environmental and cultural influences. But it is only the individuals who break through the social pattern by understanding it, and who are therefore not bound by the conditioning of their own minds—it is only such people who can bring about a new civilization, not the people who merely conform, or who resist one particular pattern because they are shaped by another. The search for God or truth does not lie within the prison, but rather in understanding the prison and breaking through its walls—and this very movement toward freedom creates a new culture, a different world.

Questioner: Sir, why do we want to have a companion?

KRISHNAMURTI: A girl asks why we want a companion. Why does one want a companion? Can you live alone in this world without a husband or a wife, without children, without friends? Most people cannot live alone, therefore they need companions. It requires enormous intelligence to be alone; and you *must* be alone to find God, truth. It is nice to have a companion, a husband or a wife, and also to have babies; but you see, we get lost in all that, we get lost in the family, in the job, in the dull, monotonous routine of a decaying existence. We get used to it, and then the thought of living alone becomes dreadful, something to be afraid of. Most of us have put all our faith in one thing, all our eggs in one basket, and our lives have no richness apart from our companions, apart from our families and our jobs. But if there is richness in one's life—not the richness of money or knowledge, which anyone can acquire, but that richness which is the movement of reality with no beginning and no ending—then companionship becomes a secondary matter.

But, you see, you are not educated to be alone. Do you ever go out for a walk by yourself? It is very important to go out alone, to sit under a tree—not with a book, not with a companion, but by yourself—and observe the falling of a leaf, hear the lapping of the water, the fisherman's song, watch the flight of a bird, and of your own thoughts as they chase each other across the space of your mind. If you are able to be alone and watch these things, then you will discover extraordinary riches which no government can tax, no human agency can corrupt, and which can never be destroyed.

Questioner: Is it your hobby to give lectures? Don't you get tired of talking? Why are you doing it?

KRISHNAMURTI: I am glad you asked that question. You know, if you love something, you never get tired of it—I mean love in which there is no seeking of a result, no wanting something out of it. When you love something, it is not self-fulfilment, therefore there is no disappointment, there is no end. Why am I doing this? You might as well ask why the rose blooms, why the jasmine gives its scent, or why the bird flies.

You see, I have tried *not* talking, to find out what happens if I don't talk. That is all right too. Do you understand? If you are talking because you are getting something out of it—money, a reward, a sense of your own importance—then there is weariness, then your talking is destructive, it has no meaning because it is only self-fulfilment; but if there is love in your heart, and your heart is not filled with the things of the mind, then it is like a fountain, like a spring that is timelessly giving fresh water.

Questioner: When I love a person and he gets angry, why is his anger so intense?

KRISHNAMURTI: First of all, do you love anybody? Do you know what it is to love? It is to give completely your mind, your heart, your whole being and not ask a thing in return, not put out a begging bowl to receive love. Do you understand? When there is that kind of love, is there anger? And why do we get angry when we love somebody with the ordinary, so-called love? It is because we are not getting something we expect from that person, is it not? I love my wife or husband, my son or daughter, but the moment they do something "wrong" I get angry. Why?

Why does the father get angry with his son or daughter? Because he wants the child to be or do something, to fit into a certain pattern, and the child rebels. Parents try to fulfil, to immortalize themselves through their property, through their children and, when the child does something of which they disapprove, they get violently angry. They have an ideal of what the child should be, and through that ideal they are fulfilling themselves; and they get angry when the child does not fit into the pattern which is their fulfilment.

Have you noticed how angry you sometimes get with a friend of yours? It is the same process going on. You are expecting something from him, and when that expectation is not fulfilled you are disappointed—which means, really, that inwardly, psychologically you are depending on that person. So wherever there is psychological dependence, there must be frustration; and frustration inevitably breeds anger, bitterness, jealousy, and various other forms of conflict. That is why it is very important, especially while you are young, to love something with your whole being—a tree, an animal, your teacher, your parent—for then you will find out for yourself what it is to be without conflict, without fear.

But you see, the educator is generally concerned about himself, he is caught up in his personal worries about his family, his money, his position. He has no love in his heart, and this is one of the difficulties in education. *You* may have love in your heart, because to love is a natural thing when one is young; but it is soon destroyed by the parents, by the educator, by the social environment. To maintain that innocence, that love which is the perfume of life, is extraordinarily arduous; it requires a great deal of intelligence, insight.

Questioner: How can the mind go beyond its hindrances?

KRISHNAMURTI: To go beyond its hindrances, the mind must first be aware of them, must it not? You must know the limitations, the boundaries, the frontiers of your own mind; but very few of us know them. We say that we do, but it is merely a verbal assertion. We never say, "Here is a barrier, a bondage within me, and I want to understand it; therefore I am going to be cognizant of it, see how it came into being and the whole nature of it". If one knows what the disease is, there is a possibility of curing it. But to know the disease, to know the particular limitation, bondage or hindrance of the mind, and to understand it, one must not condemn it, one must not say it is right or wrong. One must observe it without having an opinion, a prejudice about it—which is extraordinarily difficult, because we are brought up to condemn.

To understand a child, there must be no condemnation. To condemn him has no meaning. You have to watch him when he is playing, crying, eating, you have to observe him in all his moods; but you cannot do this if you say he is ugly, he is stupid, he is this or that. Similarly, if one can watch the hindrances of the mind, not only the superficial hindrances but also the deeper hindrances in the unconscious—watch them without condemnation—then the mind can go beyond them; and that very going beyond is a movement towards truth.

Questioner: Why has God created so many men and women in the world?

KRISHNAMURTI: Why do you take it for granted that God has created us? There is a very simple explanation:

the biological instinct. Instinct, desire, passion, lust are all part of life. If you say, "Life is God," then that is a different matter. Then God is everything, including passion, lust, envy, fear. All these factors have gone to produce in the world an overwhelming number of men and women, so there is the problem of over-population, which is one of the curses of this land. But you see, this problem is not so easily solved. There are various urges and compulsions which man is heir to and, without understanding that whole complex process, merely to try to regulate the birth rate has not much significance. We have made a mess of this world, each one of us, because we don't know what living is. Living is not this tawdry, mediocre, disciplined thing which we call our existence. Living is something entirely different; it is abundantly rich, timelessly changing, and as long as we don't understand that eternal movement, our lives are bound to have very little meaning.

13

Equality and Freedom

Rain on dry land is an extraordinary thing, is it not? It washes the leaves clean, the earth is refreshed. And I think we all ought to wash our minds completely clean, as the trees are washed by the rain, because they are so heavily laden with the dust of many centuries, the dust of what we call knowledge, experience. If you and I would cleanse the mind every day, free it of yesterday's reminiscences, each one of us would then have a fresh mind, a mind capable of dealing with the many problems of existence.

Now, one of the great problems that is disturbing the world is what is called equality. In one sense there is no such thing as equality, because we all have many different capacities; but we are discussing equality in the sense that all people should be treated alike. In a school, for example, the positions of the principal, the teachers and the house parents are merely jobs, functions; but, you see, with certain jobs or functions goes what is called status, and status is respected because it implies power, prestige, it means being in a position to tell people off, to order people about, to give jobs to one's friends and the members of one's family. So with function goes status; but if we could remove this whole idea of status, of power, of position, prestige, of giving benefits to others, then function would have quite a different and simple meaning, would it not? Then, whether people were governors, prime ministers, cooks, or poor teachers, they would all be treated with the same respect because they are all performing a different but necessary function in society.

Do you know what would happen, especially in a school, if we could really remove from function the whole sense of power, of position, prestige; the feeling, "I am the Head, I am important"? We would all be living in quite a different atmosphere, would we not? There would be no authority in the sense of the high and the low, the big man and the little man, and therefore there would be freedom. And it is very important that we create such an atmosphere in the school, an atmosphere of freedom in which there is love, in which each one feels a tremendous sense of confidence; because, you see, confidence comes when you feel completely at home, secure. Do you feel at ease in your own home if your father, your mother and your grandmother are constantly telling you what to do so that you gradually lose all confidence in doing anything by yourself? As you grow up you must be able to discuss, to find out if what you think is true and stick to it. You must be able to stand by something which you feel is right, even though it brings pain, suffering, loss of money, and all the rest of it; and for that you must feel, while you are young, completely secure and at ease.

Most young people don't feel secure because they are frightened. They are afraid of their elders, of their teachers, of their mothers and fathers, so they never really feel at home. But when you *do* feel at home, there happens a very strange thing. When you can go to your room, lock the door and be there by yourself unnoticed, with no one telling you what to do, you feel completely secure; and then you begin to flower, to understand, to unfold. To help you unfold is the function of a school;

and if it does not help you to unfold, it is no school at all.

When you feel at home in a place in the sense that you feel secure, not beaten down, not compelled to do this or that, when you feel very happy, completely at ease, then you are not naughty, are you? When you are really happy, you don't want to hurt anybody, you don't want to destroy anything. But to make the student feel completely happy is extraordinarily difficult, because he comes to the school with an idea that the principal, the teachers and the house parents are going to tell him what to do and push him around, and hence there is fear.

Most of you come from homes or from schools in which you have been educated to respect status. Your father and mother have status, the principal has status, so you come here with fear, respecting status. But we must create in the school a real atmosphere of freedom, and that can come about only when there is function without status, and therefore a feeling of equality. The real concern of right education is to help you to be a vital, sensitive human being, one who is not afraid and who has no false sense of respect because of status.

Questioner: Why do we find pleasure in our games and not in our studies?

KRISHNAMURTI: For the very simple reason that your teachers do not know how to teach. That is all, there is no very complicated reason for it. You know, if a teacher loves mathematics, or history, or whatever it is he teaches, then you also will love that subject, because love of something communicates itself. Don't you know that? If a musician loves to sing and his whole being is in it, doesn't that feeling communicate itself to you who are listening? You feel that you too would like to learn how to sing. But most educators don't love their subject; it has become a bore to them, a routine through which they have to go in order to earn a living. If your teachers really loved to teach, do you know what would happen to you? You would be extraordinary human beings. You would love not only your games and your studies, but also the flowers, the river, the birds, the earth, because you would have this thing vibrating in your hearts; and you would learn much more quickly, your minds would be excellent and not mediocre.

That is why it is very important to educate the educator—which is very difficult, because most educators are already well settled in their habits. But habit does not rest so heavily on the young; and if you love even one thing for itself—if you really love your games, or mathematics, or history, or painting, or singing—then you will find that intellectually you are alert, vital, and you will be very good in all your studies. After all, the mind wants to inquire, to know, because it is curious; but that curiosity is destroyed by the wrong kind of education. Therefore it is not only the student who must be educated, but also the teacher. Living is itself a process of education, a process of learning. There is an end to examinations, but there is no end to learning, and you can learn from everything if your mind is curious, alert.

Questioner: You have said that when one sees something to be false, that false thing drops away. I daily see that smoking is false, but it does not drop away.

KRISHNAMURTI: Have you ever watched grown-up people smoking, either your parents, your teachers, your neighbours, or somebody else? It has become a habit with them, has it not? They go on smoking day after day, year in and year out, and they have become slaves to the habit. Many of them realize how stupid it is to be a slave to something, and they fight the habit, they discipline themselves against it, they resist it, they try in all kinds of ways to get rid of it. But, you see, habit is a dead thing, it is an action which has become automatic, and the more one fights it the more strength one gives to it. But if the person who smokes becomes conscious of his habit, if he becomes aware of putting his hand into his pocket, bringing out the cigarette, tapping it, putting it in his mouth, lighting it and taking the first puff—if each time he goes through this routine he simply watches it without condemnation, without saying how terrible it is to smoke, then he is not giving new vitality to that particular habit. But really to drop something which has become a habit, you have to investigate it much more, which means going into the whole problem of why the mind cultivates habit—that is, why the mind is inattentive. If you clean your teeth every day while looking out of the window, the cleaning of your teeth becomes a habit; but if you always clean your teeth very carefully, giving your whole attention to it, then it does not become a habit, a routine that is thoughtlessly repeated.

Experiment with this, observe how the mind wants to go to sleep through habit and then remain undisturbed. Most people's minds are always functioning in the groove of habit, and as we grow older it gets worse. Probably you have already acquired dozens of habits. You are afraid of what will happen if you don't do as your parents say, if you don't marry as your father wants you to, so your mind is already functioning in a groove; and when you function in a groove, though you may be only ten or fifteen, you are already old, inwardly decaying. You may have a good body, but nothing else.

Your body may be young and straight, but your mind is burdened with its own weight.

So it is very important to understand the whole problem of why the mind always dwells in habits, runs in grooves, why it moves along a particular set of rails like a streetcar and is afraid to question, to inquire. If you say, "My father is a *Sikh*, therefore I am a *Sikh* and I am going to grow my hair, wear a turban"—if you say that without inquiring, without questioning, without any thought of breaking away, then you are like a machine. Smoking also makes you like a machine, a slave to habit, and it is only when you understand all this that the mind becomes fresh, young, active, alive, so that every day is a new day, every dawn reflected on the river is a joyous thing to behold.

Questioner: Why are we afraid when some of our elders are serious? And what makes them so serious?

KRISHNAMURTI: Have you ever thought about what it means to be serious? Are you ever serious? Are you always gay, always cheerful, laughing, or are there moments when you are quiet, serious—not serious *about* something, but just serious? And why should one be afraid when older people are serious? What is there to be afraid of? Are you afraid they may see something in you which you don't like in yourself? You see, most of us don't think about these matters; if we are afraid in the presence of a grave or serious older person, we don't inquire into it, we don't ask ourselves, "Why am I afraid?"

Now, what is it to be serious? Let us find out. You may be serious about very superficial things. When buying a *sari*, for example, you may give your whole attention to it, worry about it, go to ten different shops and spend all morning looking at various patterns. That is also called being serious; but such a person is serious only superficially. Then you can be serious about going to the temple every day, placing a garland there, giving money to the priests; but all that is a very false thing, is it not? Because truth or God is not in any temple. And you can be very serious about nationalism, which is another false thing.

Do you know what nationalism is? It is the feeling, "My India, my country, right or wrong", or the feeling that India has vast treasures of spiritual knowledge and is therefore greater than any other nation. When we identify ourselves with a particular country and feel proud of it, we bring about nationalism in the world. Nationalism is a false god, but millions of people are very serious about it; they will go to war, destroy, kill or be killed in the name of their country, and this kind of seriousness is used and exploited by the politicians.

So you can be serious about false things. But if you really begin to inquire into what it means to be serious, then you will find that there is a seriousness which is not measured by the activity of the false or shaped by a particular pattern—a seriousness which comes into being when the mind is not pursuing a result, an end.

Questioner: What is destiny?

KRISHNAMURTI: Do you really want to go into this problem? To ask a question is the easiest thing in the world, but your question has meaning only if it affects you directly so that you are very serious about it. Have you noticed how many people lose interest once they have asked their question? The other day a man put a question and then began to yawn, scratch his head and talk to his neighbour; he had completely lost interest. So I suggest that you don't ask a question unless you are really serious about it.

This problem of what is destiny is very difficult and complex. You see, if a cause is set going it must inevitably produce a result. If a vast number of people, whether Russians, Americans, or Hindus, prepare for war, their destiny is war; though they may say they want peace and are preparing only for their own defence, they have set in motion causes which bring about war. Similarly, when millions of people have for centuries taken part in the development of a certain civilization or culture, they have set going a movement in which individual human beings are caught up and swept along, whether they like it or not; and this whole process of being caught up in and swept along by a particular stream of culture or civilization may be called destiny.

After all, if you are born as the son of a lawyer who insists that you also become a lawyer, and if you comply with his wishes even though you would prefer to do something else, then your destiny is obviously to become a lawyer. But if you refuse to become a lawyer, if you insist upon doing that which you feel to be the true thing for you, which is what you really love to do—it may be writing, painting, or having no money and begging—then you have stepped out of the stream, you have broken away from the destiny which your father intended for you. It is the same with a culture or civilization.

That is why it is very important that we should be rightly educated—educated not to be smothered by tradition, not to fall into the destiny of a particular racial, cultural or family group, educated not to become mechanical beings moving towards a predetermined end.

The man who understand this whole process, who breaks away from it and stands alone, creates his own momentum; and if his action is a breaking away from the false towards the truth, then that momentum itself becomes the truth. Such men are free of destiny.

14
Self Discipline

Have you ever considered why we are disciplined, or why we discipline ourselves? Political parties all over the world insist that the party discipline be followed. Your parents, your teachers, the society around you—they all tell you that you must be disciplined, controlled. Why? And is there really any necessity for discipline at all? I know we are accustomed to think that discipline is necessary—the discipline imposed either by society, or by a religious teacher, or by a particular moral code, or by our own experience. The ambitious man who wants to achieve, who wants to make a lot of money, who wants to be a great politician—his very ambition becomes the means of his own discipline. So everyone around you says that discipline is necessary: you must go to bed and get up at a certain hour, you must study, pass examinations, obey your father and mother, and so on.

Now, why should you be disciplined at all? What does discipline mean? It means adjusting yourself to something, does it not? To adjust your thinking to what other people say, to resist some forms of desire and accept others, to comply with this practice and not with that, to conform, to suppress, to follow, not only on the surface of the mind, but also deep down—all this is implied in discipline. And for centuries, age after age, we have been told by teacher, *gurus*, priests, politicians, kings, lawyers, by the society in which we live, that there must be discipline.

So, I am asking myself—and I hope you too are asking yourself—whether discipline is necessary at all, and whether there is not an entirely different approach to this problem? I think there *is* a different approach, and this is the real issue which is confronting not only the schools but the whole world. You see, it is generally accepted that, in order to be efficient, you must be disciplined, either by a moral code, a political creed, or by being trained to work like a machine in a factory; but this very process of discipline is making the mind dull through conformity.

Now, does discipline set you free, or does it make you conform to an ideological pattern, whether it be the utopian pattern of communism, or some kind of moral or religious pattern? Can discipline ever set you free? Having bound you, made you a prisoner, as all forms of discipline do, can it then let you go? How can it? Or is there a different approach altogether—which is to awaken a really deep insight into the whole problem of discipline? That is, can you, the individual, have only one desire and not two or many conflicting desires? Do you understand what I mean? The moment you have two, three, or ten desires, you have the problem of discipline, have you not? You want to be rich, to have cars, houses, and at the same time you want to renounce these things because you think that to possess little or nothing is moral, ethical, religious. And is it possible to be educated in the right way so that one's whole being is integrated, without contradiction, and therefore without the need of discipline? To be integrated implies a sense of freedom, and when this integration is taking place there is surely no need for discipline. Integration means being one thing totally on all levels at the same time.

You see, if we could have right education from the

very tenderest age, it would bring about a state in which there is no contradiction at all, either within or without; and then there would be no need for discipline or compulsion because you would be doing something completely, freely, with your whole being. Discipline arises only when there is a contradiction. The politicians, the governments, the organized religions want you to have only one way of thinking, because if they can make you a complete communist, a complete Catholic, or whatever it is, then you are not a problem, you simply believe and work like a machine; then there is no contradiction because you just follow. But all following is destructive because it is mechanical, it is mere conformity in which there is no creative release.

Now, can we bring about, from the tenderest age, a sense of complete security, a feeling of being at home, so that in you there is no struggle to be *this* and not to be *that?* Because the moment there is an inward struggle there is conflict, and to overcome that conflict there must be discipline. Whereas, if you are rightly educated, then everything that you do is an integrated action; there is no contradiction and hence no compulsive action. As long as there is no integration there must be discipline, but discipline is destructive because it does not lead to freedom.

To be integrated does not demand any form of discipline. That is, if I am doing what is good, what is intrinsically true, what is really beautiful, doing it with my whole being, then there is no contradiction in me and I am not merely conforming to something. If what I am doing is totally good, right in itself—not right according to some Hindu tradition or communist theory, but timelessly right under all circumstances—then I am an integrated human being and have no need for discipline. And is it not the function of a school to bring about in you this sense of integrated confidence so that what you are doing is not merely what you wish to do, but that which is fundamentally right and good, everlastingly true?

You know, if you love there is no need for discipline, is there? Love brings its own creative understanding, therefore there is no resistance, no conflict; but to love with such complete integration is possible only when you feel deeply secure, completely at home, especially while you are young. This means, really, that the educator and the student must have abounding confidence in each other, otherwise we shall create a society which will be as ugly and destructive as the present one. If we can understand the significance of completely integrated action in which there is no contradiction, and therefore no need for discipline, then I think we shall bring about a totally different kind of culture, a new civilization. But if we merely resist, suppress, then what is suppressed will inevitably rebound in other directions and set going various mischievous activities and destructive events.

So it is very important to understand this whole question of discipline. To me, discipline is something altogether ugly; it is not creative, it is destructive. But merely to stop there, with a statement of that kind, may seem to imply that you can do whatever you like. On the contrary, a man who loves does *not* do whatever he likes. It is love alone that leads to right action. What brings order in the world is to love and let love do what it will.

Questioner: Why do we hate the poor?

KRISHNAMURTI: Do you really hate the poor? I am not condemning you; I am just asking, do you really hate the poor? And if you do, why? Is it because you also may be poor one day, and imagining your own plight then, you reject it? Or is it that you dislike the sordid, dirty, unkempt existence of the poor? Disliking untidiness, disorder, squalor, filth, you say, "I don't want to have anything to do with the poor." Is that it? But who has created poverty, squalor and disorder in the world? You, your parents, your government—our whole society has created them; because, you see, we have no love in our hearts. We love neither our children nor our neighbours, neither the living nor the dead. We have no love for anything at all. The politicians are not going to eradicate all this misery and ugliness in the world, any more than the religions and the reformers will, because they are only concerned with a little patchwork here and there; but if there were love, then all these ugly things would disappear tomorrow.

Do you love anything? Do you know what it is to love? You know, when you love something completely, with your whole being, that love is not sentimental, it is not duty, it is not divided as physical or divine. Do you love anyone or anything with your whole being—your parents, a friend, your dog, a tree? Do you? I am afraid you don't. That is why you have vast spaces in your being in which there is ugliness, hate, envy. You see, the man who loves has no room for anything else. We should really spend our time discussing all this and finding out how to remove the things that are so cluttering our minds that we cannot love; for it is only when we love that we can be free and happy. It is only people who are loving, vital, happy, that can create a new world—not the politicians, not the reformers or the few ideological saints.

Questioner: You talk about truth, goodness and integration, which implies that on the other side there is untruth, evil and disintegration. So how can one be true, good and integrated without discipline?

Krishnamurti: In other words, being envious, how can one be free of envy without discipline? I think it is very important to understand the question itself; because the answer is in the question, it is not apart from the question.

Do you know what envy means? You are nice looking, you are finely dressed, or wear a beautiful turban or *sari*, and I also want to dress like that; but I cannot, so I am envious. I am envious because I want what you have; I want to be different from what I am.

I am envious because I want to be as beautiful as you are; I want to have the fine clothes, the elegant house, the high position that you have. Being dissatisfied with what I am, I want to be like you; but, if I understood my dissatisfaction and its cause, then I would not want to be like you or long for the things that you have. In other words, if once I begin to understand what I am, then I shall never compare myself with another or be envious of anyone. Envy arises because I want to change myself and become like somebody else. But if I say, "Whatever I am, *that* I want to understand", then envy is gone; then there is no need of discipline, and out of the understanding of what I am comes integration.

Our education, our environment, our whole culture insists that we must become something. Our philosophies, our religions and sacred books all say the same thing. But now I see that the very process of becoming something implies envy, which means that I am not satisfied with being what I am; and I want to understand what I am, I want to find out why I am always comparing myself with another, trying to become something; and in understanding what I am there is no need for discipline. In the process of that understanding, integration comes into being. The contradiction in me yields to the understanding of myself, and this in turn brings an action which is integral, whole.

Questioner: What is power?

KRISHNAMURTI: There is mechanical power, the power produced by the internal combustion engine, by steam, or by electricity. There is the power that dwells in a tree, that causes the sap to flow, that creates the leaf. There is the power to think very clearly, the power to love, the power to hate, the power of a dictator, the power to exploit people in the name of God, in the name of the Masters, in the name of a country. These are all forms of power.

Now, power as electricity or light, atomic power, and so on—all such forms of power are good in themselves, are they not? But the power of the mind that uses them for the purposes of aggression and tyranny, to gain something for itself—such power is evil under all circumstances. The head of any society, church or religious group who has power over other people is an evil person, because he is controlling, shaping, guiding others without knowing where he himself is going. This is true not only of the big organizations, but of the little societies all over the world. The moment a person is clear, unconfused, he ceases to be a leader and therefore he has no power.

So it is very important to understand why the human mind demands to have power over others. The parents have power over their children, the wife over the husband, or the husband over the wife. Beginning in the small family, the evil extends until it becomes the tyranny of governments, of political leaders and religious interpreters. And can one live without this hunger for power, without wanting to influence or exploit people, without wanting power for oneself, or for a group or a nation, or for a Master or a saint? All such forms of power are destructive, they bring misery to man. Whereas, to be really kind, to be considerate, to love—this is a strange thing, it has its own timeless effect. Love is its own eternity, and where there is love there is no evil power.

Questioner: Why do we seek fame?

KRISHNAMURTI: Have you ever thought about it? We want to be famous as a writer, as a poet, as a painter, as a politician, as a singer, or what you will. Why? Because we really don't love what we are doing. If you loved to sing, or to paint, or to write poems—if you really loved it—you would not be concerned with whether you are famous or not. To want to be famous is tawdry, trivial, stupid, it has no meaning; but, because we don't love what we are doing, we want to enrich ourselves with fame. Our present education is rotten because it teaches us to love success and not what we are doing. The result has become more important than the action.

You know, it is good to hide your brilliance under a bushel, to be anonymous, to love what you are doing and not to show off. It is good to be kind without a name. That does not make you famous, it does not cause your photograph to appear in the newspapers. Politicians do not come to your door. You are just a creative human being living anonymously, and in that there is richness and great beauty.

15

Cooperation and Sharing

We have been talking of so many things, of the many problems of life, have we not? But I wonder if we really know what a problem is. Problems become difficult to solve if they are allowed to take root in the mind. The mind creates the problems, and then becomes the soil in which they take root; and once a problem is well established in the mind it is very difficult to uproot it. What is essential is for the mind itself to see the problem and not give it the soil to grow.

One of the basic problems confronting the world is the problem of cooperation. What does the word "Cooperation" mean? To cooperate is to do things together, to build together, to feel together, to have something in common so that we can freely work together. But people generally don't feel inclined to work together naturally, easily, happily; and so they are compelled to work together through various inducements: threat, fear, punishment, reward. This is the common practice throughout the world. Under tyrannical governments you are brutally forced to work together; if you don't "cooperate" you are liquidated or sent to a concentration camp. In the so-called civilized nations you are induced to work together through the concept of "my country", or for an ideology which has been very carefully worked out and widely propagated so that you accept it; or you work together to carry out a plan which somebody has drawn up, a blueprint for Utopia.

So, it is the plan, the idea, the authority which induces people to work together. This is generally called co-operation, and in it there is always the implication of reward or punishment, which means that behind such "cooperation" there is fear. You are always working *for* something—for the country, for the king, for the party, for God or the Master, for peace, or to bring about this or that reform. Your idea of cooperation is to work together for a particular result. You have an ideal—to build a perfect school, or what you will—towards which you are working, therefore you say cooperation is necessary. All this implies authority, does it not? There is always someone who is supposed to know what is the right thing to do, and therefore you say, "we must cooperate in carrying it out".

Now, I don't call that cooperation at all. That is not cooperation, it is a form of greed, a form of fear, compulsion. Behind it there is the threat that if you don't "cooperate" the government won't recognize you, or the Five Year Plan will fail, or you will be sent to a concentration camp, or your country will lose the war, or you may not go to heaven. There is always some form of inducement, and where there is inducement there cannot be real cooperation.

Nor is it cooperation when you and I work together merely because we have mutually agreed to do something. In any such agreement what is important is the doing of that particular thing, not working together. You and I may agree to build a bridge, or construct a road, or plant some trees together, but in that agreement there is always the fear of disagreement, the fear that I may not do my share and let you do the whole thing.

So it is not cooperation when we work together through any form of inducement, or by mere agreement, because behind all such effort there is the implication of gaining or avoiding something.

To me, cooperation is entirely different. Cooperation is the fun of being and doing together—not necessarily doing something in particular. Do you understand? Young children normally have a feeling for being and doing together. Haven't you noticed this? They will cooperate in anything. There is no question of agreement or disagreement, reward or punishment; they just want to help. They cooperate instinctively, for the fun of being and doing together. But grown-up people destroy this natural, spontaneous spirit of cooperation in children by saying, "If you do this I will give you that; if you don't do this I won't let you go to the cinema", which introduces the corruptive element.

So, real cooperation comes, not through merely agreeing to carry out some project together, but with the joy, the feeling of togetherness, if one may use that word; because in that feeling there is not the obstinacy of personal ideation, personal opinion.

When you know such cooperation, you will also know when *not* to cooperate, which is equally important. Do you understand? It is necessary for all of us to awaken in ourselves this spirit of cooperation, for then it will not be a mere plan or agreement which causes us to work together, but an extraordinary feeling of togetherness, the sense of joy in being and doing together without any thought of reward or punishment. That is very important. But it is equally important to know when *not* to cooperate; because if we are not wise we may cooperate with the unwise, with ambitious leaders who have grandiose schemes, fantastic ideas, like Hitler and other tyrants down through the ages. So we must know when *not* to cooperate; and we can know this only when we know the joy of real cooperation.

This is a very important question to talk over, because

when it is suggested that we work together, your immediate response is likely to be, "What for? What shall we do together?" In other words, the thing to be done becomes more important than the feeling of being and doing together; and when the thing to be done—the plan, the concept, the ideological Utopia—assumes primary importance, then there is no real cooperation. Then it is only the idea that is binding us together; and if one idea can bind us together, another idea can divide us. So, what matters is to awaken in ourselves this spirit of cooperation, this feeling of joy in being and doing together, without any thought of reward or punishment. Most young people have it spontaneously, freely, if it is not corrupted by their elders.

Questioner: How can we get rid of our mental worries if we can't avoid the situations which cause them?

KRISHNAMURTI: Then you have to face them, have you not? To get rid of worry you generally try to escape from the problem; you go to the temple or the cinema, you read a magazine, turn on the radio, or seek some other form of distraction. But escape does not solve the problem, because when you come back it is still there; so why not face it from the very beginning?

Now, what is worry? You worry about whether you will pass your examinations, and you are afraid that you won't; so you sweat over it, spend sleepless nights. If you don't pass, your parents will be disappointed; and also you would like to be able to say, "I have done it, I have passed my examinations". You go on worrying right up to examination day and until you know the results. Can you escape, run away from the situation? Actually, you can't, can you? So you have to face it. But why worry about it? You have studied, you have done your best, and you will pass or not pass. The more you worry about it the more frightened and nervous you become, and the less you are capable of thinking; and when the day arrives you cannot write a thing, you can only look at the clock—which is what happened to me!

When the mind goes over and over a problem and is ceaselessly concerned with it, that is what we call worry, is it not? Now, how is one to get rid of worry? First of all, it is important for the mind not to give soil for the problem to take root.

Do you know what the mind is? Great philosophers have spent many years in examining the nature of the mind, and books have been written about it; but, if one really gives one's whole attention to it, I think it is fairly simple to find out what the mind is. Have you ever observed your own mind? All that you have learnt up to now, the memory of all your little experiences, what you have been told by your parents, by your teachers, the things that you have read in books or observed in the world around you—all this is the mind. It is the mind that observes, that discerns, that learns, that cultivates so-called virtues, that communicates ideas, that has desires and fears. It is not only what you see on the surface, but also the deep layers of the unconscious in which are hidden the racial ambitions, motives, urges, conflicts. All this is the mind, which is called consciousness.

Now, the mind wants to be occupied with something, like a mother worrying about her children, or a housewife about her kitchen, or a politician about his popularity or his position in parliament; and a mind that is occupied is incapable of solving any problem. Do you see that? It is only the unoccupied mind that can be fresh to understand a problem.

Observe your own mind and you will see how restless it is, always occupied with something: with what somebody said yesterday, with something you have just learned, with what you are going to do tomorrow, and so on. It is never unoccupied—which does not mean a stagnant mind, or a kind of mental vacuum. As long as it is occupied, whether with the highest or the lowest, the mind is small, petty; and a petty mind can never resolve any problem, it can only be occupied with it. However big a problem may be, in being occupied with it the mind makes it petty. Only a mind that is unoccupied and therefore fresh can tackle and resolve the problem.

But it is very difficult to have an unoccupied mind. Sometimes when you are sitting quietly by the river, or in your room, observe yourself and you will see how constantly that little space of which we are conscious, and which we call the mind, is filled with the many thoughts that come precipitately into it. As long as the mind is filled, occupied with something—whether it be the mind of a housewife or of the greatest scientist—it is small, petty, and whatever problem it tackles, it cannot resolve that problem. Whereas, a mind that is unoccupied, that has space, can tackle the problem and resolve it, because such a mind is fresh, it approaches the problem anew, not with the ancient heritage of its own memories and traditions.

Questioner: How can we know ourselves?

KRISHNAMURTI: You know your face because you have often looked at it reflected in the mirror. Now, there is a mirror in which you can see yourself entirely—not your face, but all that you think, all that you feel, your motives, your appetites, your urges and fears. That mirror is the mirror of relationship: the relationship between you and your parents, between you and your teachers, between you and the river, the trees, the earth, between you and your thoughts. Relationship is a mirror in which you can see yourself, not as you would wish to be, but as you are. I may wish, when looking in an ordinary mirror, that it would show me to be beautiful, but that does not happen because the mirror reflects my face exactly as it is and I cannot deceive myself. Similarly, I can see myself exactly as I am in the mirror of my relationship with others. I can observe how I talk to people: most politely to those who I think can give me something, and rudely or contemptuously to those who cannot. I am attentive to those I am afraid of. I get up when important people come in, but when the servant enters I pay no attention. So, by observing myself in relationship, I have found out how falsely I respect people, have I not? And I can also discover myself as I am in my relationship with the trees and the birds, with ideas and books.

You may have all the academic degrees in the world, but if you don't know yourself you are a most stupid person. To know oneself is the very purpose of all education. Without self-knowledge, merely to gather facts or take notes so that you can pass examinations is a stupid way of existence. You may be able to quote the *Bhagavad Gita*, the *Upanishads*, the *Koran* and the Bible, but unless you know yourself you are like a parrot repeating words. Whereas, the moment you begin to know yourself, however little, there is already set going an extraordinary process of creativeness. It is a discovery to suddenly see yourself as you actually are: greedy, quarrelsome, angry, envious, stupid. To see the fact without trying to alter it, just to see exactly what you are is an astonishing revelation. From there you can go deeper and deeper, infinitely, because there is no end to self-knowledge.

Through self-knowledge you begin to find out what is God, what is truth, what is that state which is timeless. Your teacher may pass on to you the knowledge which he received from *his* teacher, and you may do well in your examinations, get a degree and all the rest of it; but, without knowing yourself as you know your own face in the mirror, all other knowledge has very little meaning. Learned people who don't know themselves are really unintelligent; they don't know what thinking is, what life is. That is why it is important for the educator to be educated in the true sense of the word, which means that he must know the workings of his own mind and heart, see himself exactly as he is in the mirror of relationship. Self-knowledge is the beginning of wisdom. In self-knowledge is the whole universe; it embraces all the struggles of humanity.

Questioner: Can we know ourselves without an inspirer?

KRISHNAMURTI: To know yourself must you have an inspirer, somebody to urge, stimulate, push you on? Listen to the question very carefully and you will discover the true answer. You know, half the problem is solved if you study it, is it not? But you cannot study the problem fully if your mind is occupied too eagerly with finding an answer.

The question is: in order to have self-knowledge must there not be someone to inspire us?

Now, if you must have a *guru*, somebody to inspire you, to encourage you, to tell you that you are doing well, it means that you are relying on that person, and inevitably you are lost when he goes away someday. The moment you depend on a person or an idea for inspiration there is bound to be fear, therefore it is not true inspiration at all. Whereas, if you watch a dead body being carried away, or observe two people quarrelling, does it not make you think? When you see somebody being very ambitious, or notice how you all fall at the feet of your governor when he comes in, does it not make you reflect? So there is inspiration in everything, from the falling of a leaf or the death of a bird to man's own behaviour. If you watch all these things you are learning all the time; but if you look to one person as your teacher, then you are lost and that person becomes your nightmare. That is why it is very important not to follow anybody, not to have one particular teacher, but to learn from the river, the flowers, the trees, from the woman who carries a burden, from the members of your family and from your own thoughts. This is an education which nobody can give you but yourself, and that is the beauty of it. It demands ceaseless watchfulness, a constantly inquiring mind. You have to learn by observing, by struggling, by being happy and tearful.

Questioner: With all the contradictions in oneself, how is it possible to be and to do simultaneously?

KRISHNAMURTI: Do you know what self-contradiction is? If I want to do a particular thing in life and at the same time I want to please my parents, who would like me to do something else, there is in me a conflict, a contradiction. Now, how am I to resolve it? If I cannot resolve this contradiction in myself, there can obviously be no integration of being and doing. So the first thing is to be free of self-contradiction.

Suppose you want to study painting because to paint is the joy of your life, and your father says that you must become a lawyer or a business man, otherwise he will cut you off and not pay for your education; there is then a contradiction in you, is there not? Now, how are you to remove that inner contradiction, to be free of the struggle and the pain of it? As long as you are caught in self-contradiction you cannot think; so you must remove the contradiction, you must do one thing or the other. Which will it be? Will you yield to your father? If you do, it means that you have put away your joy, you have wed something which you do not love; and will that resolve the contradiction? Whereas, if you withstand your father, if you say, "Sorry, I don't care if I have to beg, starve, I am going to paint," then there is no contradiction; then being and doing are simultaneous, because you know what you want to do and you do it with your whole heart. But if you become a lawyer or a business man while inside you are burning to be a painter, then for the rest of your life you will be a dull, weary human being living in torment, in frustration, in misery, being destroyed and destroying others.

This is a very important problem for you to think out, because as you grow up your parents are going to want you to do certain things, and if you are not very clear in yourself about what you really want to do you will be led like a sheep to the slaughter. But if you find out what it is you love to do and give your whole life to it, then there is no contradiction, and in that state your being is your doing.

Questioner: For the sake of what we love to do should we forget our duty to our parents?

KRISHNAMURTI: What do you mean by that extraordinary word "duty"? Duty to whom? To your parents, to the government, to society? If your parents say it is your duty to become a lawyer and properly support them, and you really want to be a *sannyasi*, what will you do? In India to be a *sannyasi* is safe and respectable, so your father may agree. When you put on the ascetic's robe you have already become a great man, and your father can trade on it. But if you want to work with your hands, if you want to be a simple carpenter or a maker of beautiful things of clay, then where does your duty lie? Can anyone tell you? Must you not think it out very carefully for yourself, seeing all the implications involved, so that you can say, "This I feel is the right thing for me to do and I shall stick to it whether my parents agree or not?" Not merely to comply with what your parents and society want you to do, but really to think out the implications of duty; to see very clearly what is true and stick to it right through life, even though it may mean starvation, misery, death—to do that requires a great deal of intelligence, perception, insight, and also a great deal of love. You see, if you support your parents merely because you think it is your duty, then your support is a thing of the market place, without deep significance, because in it there is no love.

Questioner: However much I may want to be an engineer, if my father is against it and won't help me, how can I study engineering?

KRISHNAMURTI: If you persist in wanting to be an engineer even though your father turns you out of the house, do you mean to say that you won't find ways and means to study engineering? You will beg, go to friends. Sir, life is very strange. The moment you are very clear about what you want to do, things happen. Life comes to your aid—a friend, a relation, a teacher, a grandmother, somebody helps you. But if you are afraid to try because your father may turn you out, then you are lost. Life never comes to the aid of those who merely yield to some demand out of fear. But if you say, "This is what I really want to do and I am going to pursue it," then you will find that something miraculous takes place. You may have to go hungry, struggle to get through, but you will be a worthwhile human being, not a mere copy, and that is the miracle of it.

You see, most of us are frightened to stand alone; and I know this is especially difficult for you who are young, because there is no economic freedom in this country as there is in America or Europe. Here the country is over-populated, so everybody gives in. You say, "What will happen to me?" But if you hold on, you will find that something or somebody helps you. When you really stand against the popular demand, then you are an individual and life comes to your aid.

You know, in biology there is a phenomenon called the sport, which is a sudden and spontaneous deviation from the type. If you have a garden and have cultivated a particular species of flower, one morning you may find that something totally new has come out of that species. That new thing is called the sport. Being new it stands out, and the gardener takes a special interest in it. And life is like that. The moment you venture out, something takes place in you and about you. Life comes to your aid in various ways. You may not like the form in which it comes to you—it may be misery, struggle, starvation—but when you invite life, things begin to happen. But you see, we don't want to invite life, we want to play a safe game; and those who play a safe game die very safely. Is that not so?

16

Renewing the Mind

The other morning I saw a dead body being carried away to be burnt. It was wrapped in bright magenta cloth and it swayed with the rhythm of the four mortals who were carrying it. I wonder what kind of impression a dead body makes on one. Don't you wonder why there is deterioration? You buy a brand new motor, and within a few years it is worn out. The body also wears out; but don't you inquire a little further to find out why the mind deteriorates? Sooner or later there is the death of the body, but most of us have minds which are already dead. Deterioration has already taken place; and why does the mind deteriorate? The body deteriorates because we are constantly using it and the physical organism wears out. Disease, accident, old age, bad food, poor heredity—these are the factors which cause the deterioration and death of the body. But why should the mind deteriorate, become old, heavy, dull?

When you see a dead body, have you never wondered about this? Though our bodies must die, why should the mind ever deteriorate? Has this question never occurred to you? For the mind *does* deteriorate—we see it not only in old people, but also in the young. We see in the young how the mind is already becoming dull, heavy, insensitive; and if we can find out why the mind deteriorates, then perhaps we shall discover something really indestructible. We may understand what is eternal life, the life that is unending, that is not of time, the life that is incorruptible, that does not decay like the body which is carried to the *ghats*, burnt and the remains thrown into the river.

Now, why does the mind deteriorate? Have you ever thought about it? Being still very young—and if you have not already been made dull by society, by your parents, by circumstances—you have a fresh, eager, curious mind. You want to know why the stars exist, why the birds die, why the leaves fall, how the jet plane flies; you want to know so many things. But that vital urge to inquire, to find out, is soon smothered, is it not? It is smothered by fear, by the weight of tradition, by our own incapacity to face this extraordinary thing called life. Haven't you noticed how quickly your eagerness is destroyed by a sharp word, by a disparaging gesture, by the fear of an examination or the threat of a parent—which means that sensitivity is already being pushed aside and the mind made dull?

Another cause of dullness is imitation. You are made to imitate by tradition. The weight of the past drives you to conform, toe the line, and through conformity the mind feels safe, secure; it establishes itself in a well-oiled groove so that it can run smoothly without disturbance, without a quiver of doubt. Watch the grown-up people about you and you will see that their minds do not want to be disturbed. They want peace, even though it is the peace of death; but real peace is something entirely different.

When the mind establishes itself in a groove, in a pattern, haven't you noticed that it is always prompted by the desire to be secure? That is why it follows an ideal, an example, a *guru*. It wants to be safe, undisturbed, therefore it imitates. When you read in your history books about great leaders, saints, warriors, don't you find yourself wanting to copy them? Not that there aren't great people in the world; but the instinct is to imitate great people, to try to become like them, and that is one of the factors of deterioration because the mind then sets itself in a mould.

Furthermore, society does not want individuals who are alert, keen, revolutionary, because such individuals will not fit into the established social pattern and they may break it up. That is why society seeks to hold your mind in its pattern, and why your so-called education encourages you to imitate, to follow, to conform.

Now, can the mind stop imitating? That is, can it cease to form habits? And can the mind, which is already caught in habit, be free of habit?

The mind is the result of habit, is it not? It is the result of tradition, the result of time—time being repetition, a continuity of the past. And can the mind, *your* mind, stop thinking in terms of what has been—and of what will be, which is really a projection of what has been? Can your mind be free from habits and from creating habits? If you go into this problem very deeply you will find that it can; and when the mind renews itself without forming new patterns, habits, without again falling into the groove of imitation, then it remains fresh, young, innocent, and is therefore capable of infinite understanding.

For such a mind there is no death because there is no longer a process of accumulation. It is the process of accumulation that creates habit, imitation, and for the mind that accumulates there is deterioration, death. But a mind that is not accumulating, not gathering, that is dying each day, each minute—for such a mind there is no death. It is in a state of infinite space.

So the mind must die to everything it has gathered—to all the habits, the imitated virtues, to all the things it has relied upon for its sense of security. Then it is no longer caught in the net of its own thinking. In dying to the past from moment to moment the mind is made fresh, therefore it can never deteriorate or set in motion the wave of darkness.

Questioner: How can we put into practice what you are telling us?

KRISHNAMURTI: You hear something which you think is right and you want to carry it out in your everyday life; so there is a gap between what you think and what you do, is there not? You think one thing, and you are doing something else. But you want to put into practice what you think, so there is this gap between action and thought; and then you ask how to bridge the gap, how to link your thinking to your action.

Now, when you want to do something very much, you do it, don't you? When you want to go and play cricket, or do some other thing in which you are really interested, you find ways and means of doing it; you never ask how to put it into practice. You do it because you are eager, because your whole being, your mind and heart are in it.

But in this other matter you have become very cunning, you think one thing and do another. You say, "That is an excellent idea and intellectually I approve, but I don't know what to do about it, so please tell me how to put it into practice"—which means that you don't want to do it at all. What you really want is to postpone action, because you like to be a little bit envious, or whatever it is. You say, "Everybody else is envious, so why not I?", and you just go on as before. But if you really don't want to be envious and you see the truth of envy as you see the truth of a cobra, then you cease to be envious and that is the end of it; you never ask how to be free of envy.

So what is important is to see the truth of something, and not ask how to carry it out—which really means that you don't see the truth of it. When you meet a cobra on the road you don't ask, "What am I to do?" You understand very well the danger of a cobra and you stay away from it. But you have never really examined all the implications of envy; nobody has ever talked to you about it, gone into it very deeply with you. You have been told that you must not be envious, but you have never looked into the nature of envy; you have never observed how society and all the organized religions are built on it, on the desire to become something. But the moment you go into envy and really see the truth of it, envy drops away.

To ask, "How am I to do it?" is a thoughtless question, because when you are really interested in something which you don't know how to do, you go at it and soon begin to find out. If you sit back and say, "Please tell me a practical way to get rid of greed," you will continue to be greedy. But if you inquire into greed with an alert mind, without any prejudice, and if you put your whole being into it, you will discover for yourself the truth of greed; and it is the truth that frees you, not your looking for a way to be free.

Questioner: Why are our desires never fully realized? Why are there always hindrances that prevent us from doing completely as we wish?

KRISHNAMURTI: If your desire to do something is complete, if your whole being is in it without seeking a result, without wanting to fulfil—which means without fear

—then there is no hindrance. There is a hindrance, a contradiction only when your desire is incomplete, broken up: you want to do something and at the same time you are afraid to do it, or you half want to do something else. Besides, can you ever fully realize your desires? Do you understand? I will explain.

Society, which is the collective relationship between man and man, does not want you to have a complete desire, because if you did you would be a nuisance, a danger to society. You are permitted to have respectable desires like ambition, envy—that is perfectly all right. Being made up of human beings who are envious, ambitious, who believe and imitate, society accepts envy, ambition, belief, imitation, even though these are all intimations of fear. As long as your desires fit into the established pattern, you are a respectable citizen. But the moment you have a complete desire, which is not of the pattern, you become a danger; so society is always watching to prevent you from having a complete desire, a desire which would be the expression of your total being and therefore bring about a revolutionary action.

The action of being is entirely different from the action of becoming. The action of being is so revolutionary that society rejects it and concerns itself exclusively with the action of becoming, which is respectable because it fits into the pattern. But any desire that expresses itself in the action of becoming, which is a form of ambition, has no fulfilment. Sooner or later it is thwarted, impeded, frustrated, and we revolt against that frustration in mischievous ways.

This is a very important question to go into, because as you grow older you will find that your desires are never really fulfilled. In fulfilment there is always the shadow of frustration, and in your heart there is not a song but a cry. The desire to become—to become a great man, a great saint, a great this or that—has no end and therefore no fulfilment; its demand is ever for the "more", and such desire always breeds agony, misery, wars. But when one is free of all desire to become, there is a state of being whose action is totally different. It is. That which is has no time. It does not think in terms of fulfilment. Its very being is its fulfilment.

Questioner: I see that I am dull, but others say I am intelligent. Which should affect me: my seeing or their saying?

KRISHNAMURTI: Now, listen to the question very carefully, very quietly, don't try to find an answer. If you say that I am an intelligent man, and I know very well that I am dull, will what you say affect me? It will if I am trying to be intelligent, will it not? Then I shall be flattered, influenced by your remark. But if I see that a dull person can never cease to be dull by trying to be intelligent, then what happens?

Surely, if I am stupid and I try to be intelligent, I shall go on being stupid, because trying to be or to become something is part of stupidity. A stupid person may acquire the trimmings of cleverness, he may pass a few examinations, get a job, but he does not thereby cease to be stupid. (Please follow this, it is not a cynical statement.) But the moment a person is aware that he is dull, stupid, and instead of trying to be intelligent he begins to examine and understand his stupidity—in that moment there is the awakening of intelligence.

Take greed. Do you know what greed is? It is eating more food than you need, wanting to outshine others at games, wanting to have more property, a bigger car than someone else. Then you say that you must *not* be greedy, so you practise non-greed—which is really silly, because greed can never cease by trying to become non-greed. But if you begin to understand all the implications of greed, if you give your mind and heart to finding the truth of it, then you are free from greed as well as from its opposite. Then you are a really intelligent human being, because you are tackling what *is* and not imitating what *should* be.

So, if you are dull, don't try to be intelligent or clever, but understand what it is that is making you dull. Imitation, fear, copying somebody, following an example or an ideal—all this makes the mind dull. When you stop following, when you have no fear, when you are capable of thinking clearly for yourself—are you not then the brightest of human beings? But if you are dull and try to be clever you will join the ranks of those who are pretty dull in their cleverness.

Questioner: Why are we naughty?

KRISHNAMURTI: If you ask yourself this question when you are naughty, then it has significance, it has meaning. But when you are angry, for example, you never ask why you are angry, do you? It is only afterwards that you ask this question. Having been angry, you say, "How stupid, I should not have been angry." Whereas, if you are aware, thoughtful at the moment of anger without condemning it, if you are "all there" when the turmoil comes up in your mind, then you will see how quickly it fades away.

Children are naughty at a certain age, and they should be, because they are full of beans, life, ginger, and it has to break out in some form or other. But you see, this is really a complex question, because naughtiness may be due to wrong food, a lack of sleep, or a feeling of insecurity, and so on. If all the factors involved are not properly understood, then naughtiness on the part of children becomes a revolt within society, in which there is no release for them.

Do you know what "delinquent" children are? They are children who do all kinds of terrible things; they are in revolt within the prison of society because they have never been helped to understand the whole problem of existence. They are so vital, and some of them are extraordinarily intelligent, and their revolt is a way of saying, "Help us to understand, to break through this compulsion, this terrible conformity". That is why this question is very important for the educator, who needs educating more than the children.

Questioner: I am used to drinking tea. One teacher says it is a bad habit, and another says it is all right.

KRISHNAMURTI: What do *you* think? Put aside for the moment what other people say, it may be their prejudice, and listen to the question. What do you think of a young boy being "used" to something already—drinking tea, smoking, competitive eating, or whatever it is? It may be all right to have fallen into a habit of doing something when you are seventy or eighty, with one foot in the grave; but you are just beginning your life, and already to be used to something is a terrible thing, is it not? That is the important question, not whether you should drink tea.

You see, when you have become used to something, your mind is already on its way to the graveyard. If you think as a Hindu, a communist, a Catholic, a Protestant, then your mind is already going down, deteriorating. But if your mind is alert, inquiring to find out why you are caught in a certain habit, why you think in a particular way, then the secondary question of whether you should smoke or drink tea can be dealt with.

17

The River of Life

I don't know if on your walks you have noticed a long, narrow pool beside the river. Some fishermen must have dug it, and it is not connected with the river. The river is flowing steadily, deep and wide, but this pool is heavy with scum because it is not connected with the life of the river, and there are no fish in it. It is a stagnant pool, and the deep river, full of life and vitality, flows swiftly along.

Now, don't you think human beings are like that? They dig a little pool for themselves away from the swift current of life, and in that little pool they stagnate, die; and this stagnation, this decay we call existence. That is, we all want a state of permanency; we want certain desires to last for ever, we want pleasures to have no end. We dig a little hole and barricade ourselves in it with our families, with our ambitions, our cultures, our fears, our gods, our various forms of worship, and there we die, letting life go by—that life which is impermanent, constantly changing, which is so swift, which has such enormous depths, such extraordinary vitality and beauty.

Have you not noticed that if you sit quietly on the bank of the river you hear its song—the lapping of the water, the sound of the current going by? There is always a sense of movement, an extraordinary movement towards the wider and the deeper. But in the little pool there is no movement at all, its water is stagnant. And if you observe you will see that this is what most of us want: little stagnant pools of existence away from life. We say that our pool-existence is right, and we have invented a philosophy to justify it; we have developed social, political, economic and religious theories in support of it, and we don't want to be disturbed because, you see, what we are after is a sense of permanency.

Do you know what it means to seek permanency? It means wanting the pleasurable to continue indefinitely, and wanting that which is not pleasurable to end as quickly as possible. We want the name that we bear to be known and to continue through family, through property. We want a sense of permanency in our relationships, in our activities, which means that we are seeking a lasting, continuous life in the stagnant pool; we don't want any real changes there, so we have built a society which guarantees us the permanency of property, of name, of fame.

But you see, life is not like that at all; life is not permanent. Like the leaves that fall from a tree, all things are impermanent, nothing endures; there is always change and death. Have you ever noticed a tree standing naked against the sky, how beautiful it is? All its branches are outlined, and in its nakedness there is a poem, there is a song. Every leaf is gone and it is waiting for the spring. When the spring comes it again fills the tree with the music of many leaves, which in due season fall and are blown away; and that is the way of life.

But we don't want anything of that kind. We cling to our children, to our traditions, to our society, to our names and our little virtues, because we want permanency; and that is why we are afraid to die. We are afraid to lose the things we know. But life is not what we would like it to be; life is not permanent at all. Birds die, snow melts away, trees are cut down or destroyed by storms, and so on. But we want everything that gives us satisfaction to be permanent; we want our position, the authority we have over people, to endure. We refuse to accept life as it is in fact.

The fact is that life is like the river: endlessly moving on, ever seeking, exploring, pushing, overflowing its banks, penetrating every crevice with its water. But, you see, the mind won't allow that to happen to itself. The mind sees that it is dangerous, risky to live in a state of impermanency, insecurity, so it builds a wall around itself: the wall of tradition, of organized religion, of political and social theories. Family, name, property, the little virtues that we have cultivated—these are all within the walls, away from life. Life is moving, impermanent, and it ceaselessly tries to penetrate, to break down these walls, behind which there is a confusion and misery. The gods within the walls are all false gods, and their writings and philosophies have no meaning because life is beyond them.

Now, a mind that has no walls, that is not burdened with its own acquisitions, accumulations, with its own knowledge, a mind that lives timelessly, insecurely—to such a mind, life is an extraordinary thing. Such a mind is life itself, because life has no resting place. But most of us want a resting place; we want a little house, a name, a position, and we say these things are very important. We demand permanency and create a culture based on this demand, inventing gods which are not gods at all but merely a projection of our own desires.

A mind which is seeking permanency soon stagnates; like that pool along the river, it is soon full of corruption, decay. Only the mind which has no walls, no foothold, no barrier, no resting place, which is moving completely with life, timelessly pushing on, exploring, exploding—only such a mind can be happy, eternally new, because it is creative in itself.

Do you understand what I am talking about? You should, because all this is part of real education and, when you understand it, your whole life will be transformed, your relationship with the world, with your neighbour, with your wife or husband, will have a totally different meaning. Then you won't try to fulfil yourself through anything, seeing that the pursuit of fulfilment only invites sorrow and misery. That is why you should ask your teachers about all this and discuss it among yourselves. If you understand it, you will have begun to understand the extraordinary truth of what life is, and in that understanding there is great beauty and love, the flowering of goodness. But the efforts of a mind that is seeking a pool of security, of permanency, can only lead to darkness and corruption. Once established in the pool, such a mind is afraid to venture out, to seek, to explore; but truth, God, reality or what you will, lies beyond the pool.

Do you know what religion is? It is not in the chant, it is not in the performance of *puja*, or any other ritual, it is not in the worship of tin gods or stone images, it is not in the temples and churches, it is not in the reading of the Bible or the *Gita*, it is not in the repeating of a sacred name or in the following of some other superstition invented by men. None of this is religion.

Religion is the feeling of goodness, that love which is like the river, living, moving everlastingly. In that state you will find there comes a moment when there is no longer any search at all; and this ending of search is the beginning of something totally different. The search for God, for truth, the feeling of being completely good—not the cultivation of goodness, of humility, but the seeking out of something beyond the inventions and tricks of the mind, which means having a feeling for that something, living in it, being it—*that* is true religion. But you can do that only when you leave the pool you have dug for yourself and go out into the river of life. Then life has an astonishing way of taking care of you, because then there is no taking care on your part. Life carries you where it will because you are part of itself; then there is no problem of security, of what people say or don't say, and that is the beauty of life.

Questioner: What makes us fear death?

KRISHNAMURTI: Do you think a leaf that falls to the ground is afraid of death? Do you think a bird lives in fear of dying? It meets death when death comes; but it is not concerned about death, it is much too occupied with living, with catching insects, building a nest, singing a song, flying for the very joy of flying. Have you ever watched birds soaring high up in the air without a beat of their wings, being carried along by the wind? How endlessly they seem to enjoy themselves! They are not concerned about death. If death comes, it is all right, they are finished. There is no concern about what is going to happen; they are living from moment to moment, are they not? It is we human beings who are always concerned about death—because we are not living. That is the trouble: we are dying, we are not living. The old people are near the grave, and the young ones are not far behind.

You see, there is this preoccupation with death because we are afraid to lose the known, the things that we have gathered. We are afraid to lose a wife or husband, a child or a friend; we are afraid to lose what we have learnt, accumulated. If we could carry over all the things that we have gathered—our friends, our possessions, our virtues, our character—then we would not be afraid of death, would we? That is why we invent theories about death and the hereafter. But the fact is that death is an ending, and most of us are unwilling to face this fact. We don't want to leave the known; so it is our clinging to the known that creates fear in us, not the unknown. The unknown cannot be perceived by the known. But the mind, being made up of the known, says, "I am going to end", and therefore it is frightened.

Now, if you can live from moment to moment and not be concerned about the future, if you can life without the thought of tomorrow—which does not mean the superficiality of merely being occupied with today; if, being aware of the whole process of the known, you can relinquish the known, let it go completely, then you will find that an astonishing thing takes place. Try it for a day—put aside everything you know, forget it, and just see what happens. Don't carry over your worries from day to day, from hour to hour, from moment to moment; let them all go, and you will see that out of this freedom there comes an extraordinary life that includes both living and dying. Death is only the ending of something, and in that very dying there is a renewing.

Questioner: It is said that in each one of us truth is permanent and timeless; but, since our life is transitory, how can there be truth in us?

KRISHNAMURTI: You see, we have made of truth something permanent. And is truth permanent? If it is, then it is within the field of time. To say that something is permanent implies that it is continuous; and what is continuous is not truth. That is the beauty of truth: it must be discovered from moment to moment, not remembered. A remembered truth is a dead thing. Truth must be discovered from moment to moment because it is living, it is never the same; and yet each time you discover it, it is the same.

What is important is not to make a theory of truth, not to say that truth is permanent in us and all the rest of it—that is an invention of the old who are frightened both of death and of life. These marvellous theories—that truth is permanent, that you need not be afraid because you are an immortal soul, and so on—have been invented by frightened people whose minds are decaying and whose philosophies have no validity. The fact is that truth is life, and life has no permanency. Life has to be discovered from moment to moment, from day to day; it has to be *discovered*, it cannot be taken for granted. If you take it for granted that you know life, you are not living. Three meals a day, clothing, shelter, sex, your job, your amusements and your thinking process—that dull, repetitive process is not life. Life is something to be discovered; and you cannot discover it if you have not lost, if you have not put aside the things that you have found. Do experiment with what I am saying. Put aside your philosophies, your religions, your customs, your racial taboos and all the rest of it, for they are not life. If you are caught in those things you will never discover life; and the function of education, surely, is to help you to discover life all the time.

A man who says he knows is already dead. But the man who thinks, "I don't know", who is discovering, finding out, who is not seeking an end, not thinking in terms of arriving or becoming—such a man is living, and that living is truth.

Questioner: Can I get an idea of perfection?

KRISHNAMURTI: Probably you can. By speculating, inventing, projecting, by saying, "This is ugly and that is perfect", you will have an *idea* of perfection. But your idea of perfection, like your belief in God, has no meaning. Perfection is something that is lived in an unpremeditated moment, and that moment has no continuity; therefore perfection cannot be thought out, nor can a way be found to make it permanent. Only the mind that is very quiet, that is not premeditating, inventing, projecting, can know a moment of perfection, a moment that is complete.

Questioner: Why do we want to take revenge by hurting another who has hurt us?

KRISHNAMURTI: It is the instinctive, survival response, is it not? Whereas, the intelligent mind, the mind that is awake, that has thought about it very deeply, feels no desire to strike back—not because it is trying to be virtuous or to cultivate forgiveness, but because it perceives that to strike back is silly, it has no meaning at all. But you see, that requires meditation.

Questioner: I have fun in teasing others, but I myself get angry when teased.

KRISHNAMURTI: I am afraid it is the same with older people. Most of us like to exploit others, but we don't like it when we in our turn are exploited. Wanting to hurt or to annoy others is a most thoughtless state, is it not? It arises from a life of self-centeredness. Neither you nor the other fellow likes being teased, so why don't you both stop teasing? That means being thoughtful.

Questioner: What is the work of man?

KRISHNAMURTI: What do *you* think it is? Is it to study, pass examinations, get a job and do it for the rest of your life? Is it to go to the temple, join groups, launch various reforms? Is it man's work to kill animals for his own food? Is it man's work to build a bridge for the train to cross, to dig wells in a dry land, to find oil, to climb mountains, to conquer the earth and the air, to write poems, to paint, to love, to hate? Is all this the work of man? Building civilizations that come toppling down in a few centuries, bringing about wars, creating God in one's own image, killing people in the name of religion or the State, talking of peace and brotherhood while usurping power and being ruthless to others—this is what man is doing all around you, is it not? And is this the true work of man?

You can see that all this work leads to destruction and misery, to chaos and despair. Great luxuries exist side by side with extreme poverty; disease and starvation, with refrigerators and jet planes. All this is the work of man; and when you see it don't you ask yourself, "Is that all? Is there not something else which is the true work of man?" If we can find out what is the true work of man, then jet planes, washing machines, bridges, hostels will all have an entirely different meaning; but without finding out what is the true work of man, merely to indulge in reforms, in reshaping what man has already done, will lead nowhere.

So, what is the true work of man? Surely, the true work of man is to discover truth, God; it is to love and not to be caught in his own self-enclosing activities. In the very discovery of what is true there is love, and that love in man's relationship with man will create a different civilization, a new world.

Questioner: Why do we worship God?

KRISHNAMURTI: I am afraid we don't worship God. Don't laugh. You see, we don't love God; if we did love

God, there would not be this thing we call worship. We worship God because we are frightened of him; there is fear in our hearts, not love. The temple, the *puja*, the sacred thread—these things are not of God, they are the creations of man's vanity and fear. It is only the unhappy, the frightened who worship God. Those who have wealth, position and authority are not happy people. An ambitious man is a most unhappy human being. Happiness comes only when you are free of all that—and then you do not worship God. It is the miserable, the tortured, those who are in despair that crawl to a temple; but if they put aside this so-called worship and understand their misery, then they will be happy men and women, for they will discover what truth is, what God is.

18

The Attentive Mind

Have you ever paid any attention to the ringing of the temple bells? Now, what do you listen to? To the notes, or to the silence between the notes? If there were no silence, would there be notes? And if you listened to the silence, would not the notes be more penetrating, of a different quality? But you see, we rarely pay real attention to anything; and I think it is important to find out what it means to pay attention. When your teacher is explaining a problem in mathematics, or when you are reading history, or when a friend is talking, telling you a story, or when you are near the river and hear the lapping of the water on the bank, you generally pay very little attention; and if we could find out what it means to pay attention, perhaps learning would then have quite a different significance and become much easier.

When your teacher tells you to pay attention in class, what does he mean? He means that you must not look out of the window, that you must withdraw your attention from everything else and concentrate wholly on what you are supposed to be studying. Or, when you are absorbed in a novel, your whole mind is so concentrated on it that for the moment you have lost interest in everything else. That is another form of attention. So, in the ordinary sense, paying attention is a narrowing-down process, is it not?

Now, I think there is a different kind of attention altogether. The attention which is generally advocated, practised or indulged in is a narrowing-down of the mind to a point, which is a process of exclusion. When you make an effort to pay attention, you are really resisting something—the desire to look out of the window, to see who is coming in, and so on. Part of your energy has already gone in resistance. You build a wall around your mind to make it concentrate completely on a particular thing, and you call this the disciplining of the mind to pay attention. You try to exclude from the mind every thought but the one on which you want it to be wholly concentrated. That is what most people mean by paying attention. But I think there is a different kind of attention, a state of mind which is not exclusive, which does not shut out anything; and because there is no resistance, the mind is capable of much greater attention. But attention without resistance does not mean the attention of absorption.

The kind of attention which I would like to discuss is entirely different from what we usually mean by attention, and it has immense possibilities because it is not exclusive. When you concentrate on a subject, on a talk, on a conversation, consciously or unconsciously you build a wall of resistance against the intrusion of other thoughts, and so your mind is not wholly there; it is only partially there, however much attention you pay, because part of your mind is resisting any intrusion, any deviation or distraction.

Let us begin the other way round. Do you know what distraction is? You want to pay attention to what you are reading, but your mind is distracted by some noise outside and you look out of the window. When you want to concentrate on something and your mind wanders off, the wandering off is called distraction; then part of your mind resists the so-called distraction and there is a waste of energy in that resistance. Whereas, if you are aware of every movement of the mind from moment to moment then there is no such thing as distraction at any time and the energy of the mind is not wasted in resisting something. So it is important to find out what attention really is.

If you listen both to the sound of the bell and to the silence between its strokes, the whole of that listening is attention. Similarly, when someone is speaking, attention is the giving of your mind not only to the words but also to the silence between the words. If you experiment with this you will find that your mind can pay complete attention without distraction and without resistance. When you discipline your mind by saying, "I must not look out of the window, I must not watch the people coming in, I must pay attention even though I want to do something else", it creates a division which is very destructive because it dissipates the energy of the mind. But if you listen comprehensively so that there is no division and therefore no form of resistance then you will find that the mind can pay complete attention to anything without effort. Do you see it? Am I making myself clear?

Surely, to discipline the mind to pay attention is to bring about its deterioration—which does not mean that the mind must restlessly wander all over the place like a monkey. But, apart from the attention of absorption, these two states are all we know. Either we try to discipline the mind so tightly that it cannot deviate, or we just let it wander from one thing to another. Now, what I am describing is not a compromise between the two; on the contrary, it has nothing to do with either. It is an entirely different approach; it is to be totally aware so that your mind is all the time attentive without being caught in the process of exclusion.

Try what I am saying, and you will see how quickly

your mind can learn. You can hear a song or a sound and let the mind be so completely full of it that there is not the effort of learning. After all, if you know how to listen to what your teacher is telling you about some historical fact, if you can listen without any resistance because your mind has space and silence and is therefore not distracted, you will be aware not only of the historical fact but also of the prejudice with which he may be translating it, and of your own inward response.

I will tell you something. You know what space is. There is space in this room. The distance between here and your hostel, between the bridge and your home, between this bank of the river and the other—all that is space. Now, is there also space in your mind? Or is it so crowded that there is no space in it at all? If your mind has space, then in that space there is silence—and from that silence everything else comes, for then you can listen, you can pay attention without resistance. That is why it is very important to have space in the mind. If the mind is not overcrowded, not ceaselessly occupied, then it can listen to that dog barking, to the sound of a train crossing the distant bridge, and also be fully aware of what is being said by a person talking here. Then the mind is a living thing, it is not dead.

Questioner: Yesterday after the meeting we saw you watching two peasant children, typically poor, playing by the roadside. We would like to know what sentiments arose in your mind while you were looking at them.

KRISHNAMURTI: Yesterday afternoon several of the students met me on the road, and soon after I left them I saw the gardener's two children playing. The questioner wants to know what feelings I had while I was watching those two children.

Now, what feelings do *you* have when you observe

poor children? That is more important to find out than what I may have felt. Or are you always so busy going to your hostel or to your class that you never observe them at all?

Now, when you observe those poor women carrying a heavy load to the market, or watch the peasant children playing in the mud with very little else to play with, who will not have the education that you are getting, who have no proper home, no cleanliness, insufficient clothing, inadequate food—when you observe all that, what is your reaction? It is very important to find out for yourself what your reaction is. I will tell you what mine was.

Those children have no proper place to sleep; the father and the mother are occupied all day long, with never a holiday; the children never know what it is to be loved, to be cared for; the parents never sit down with them and tell them stories about the beauty of the earth and the heavens. And what kind of society is it that has produced these circumstances—where there are immensely rich people who have everything on earth they want, and at the same time there are boys and girls who have nothing? What kind of society is it, and how has it come into being? You may revolutionize, break the pattern of this society, but in the very breaking of it a new one is born which is again the same thing in another form—the commissars with their special houses in the country, the privileges, the uniforms, and so on down the line. This had happened after very revolution, the French, the Russian and the Chinese. And is it possible to create a society in which all this corruption and misery does not exist? It can be created only when you and I as individuals break away from the collective, when we are free of ambition and know what it means to love. That was my whole reaction, in a flash.

But did you listen to what I said?

Questioner: How can the mind listen to several things at the same time?

Krishnamurti: That is not what I was talking about. There are people who can concentrate on many things at the same time—which is merely a matter of training the mind. I am not talking about that at all. I am talking about a mind that has no resistance, that can listen because it has the space, the silence from which all thought can spring.

Questioner: Why do we like to be lazy?

Krishnamurti: What is wrong with laziness? What is wrong with just sitting still and listening to a distant sound come nearer and nearer? Or lying in bed of a morning and watching the birds in a nearby tree, or a single leaf dancing in the breeze when all the other leaves are very still? What is wrong with that? We condemn laziness because we think it is wrong to be lazy; so let us find out what we mean by laziness. If you are feeling well and yet stay in bed after a certain hour, some people may call you lazy. If you don't want to play or study because you lack energy, or for other health reasons, that again may be called laziness by somebody. But what really is laziness?

When the mind is unaware of its reactions, of its own subtle movements, such a mind is lazy, ignorant. If you can't pass examinations, if you haven't read many books and have very little information, that is not ignorance. Real ignorance is having no knowledge of yourself, no perception of how your mind works, of what your motives, your responses are. Similarly, there is laziness when the mind is asleep. And most people's minds *are* asleep. They are drugged by knowledge, by the Scriptures, by what Shankara or somebody else has said. They follow a philosophy, practise a discipline, so their minds—which should be rich, full, overflowing like the river—are made narrow, dull, weary. Such a mind is lazy. And a mind that is ambitious, that pursues a result, is not active in the true sense of the word; though it may be superficially active, pushing, working all day to get what it wants, underneath it is heavy with despair, with frustration.

So one must be very watchful to find out if one is really lazy. Don't just accept it if people tell you that you are lazy. Find out for yourself what laziness is. The man who merely accepts, rejects or imitates, the man who, being afraid, digs a little rut for himself—such a man is lazy and therefore his mind deteriorates, goes to pieces. But a man who is watchful is not lazy, even though he may often sit very quietly and observe the trees, the birds, the people, the stars and the silent river.

Questioner: You say that we should revolt against society, and at the same time you say that we should not have ambition. Is not the desire to improve society an ambition?

KRISHNAMURTI: I have very carefully explained what I mean by revolt, but I shall use two different words to make it much clearer. To revolt within society in order to make it a little better, to bring about certain reforms, is like the revolt of prisoners to improve their life within the prison walls; and such revolt is no revolt at all, it is just mutiny. Do you see the difference? Revolt within society is like the mutiny of prisoners who want better food, better treatment within the prison; but revolt born of understanding is an individual breaking away from society, and that is creative revolution.

Now, if you as an individual break away from society, is that action motivated by ambition? If it is, then you have not broken away at all, you are still within the prison, because the very basis of society is ambition, acquisitiveness, greed. But if you understand all that and bring about a revolution in your own heart and mind, then you are no longer ambitious, you are no longer motivated by envy, greed, acquisitiveness, and therefore you will be entirely outside of a society which is based on those things. Then you are a creative individual and in your action there will be the seed of a different culture.

So there is a vast difference between the action of creative revolution, and the action of revolt or mutiny within society. As long as you are concerned with mere reform, with decorating the bars and walls of the prison, you are not creative. Reformation always needs further reform, it only brings more misery, more destruction. Whereas, the mind that understands this whole structure of acquisitiveness, of greed, of ambition and breaks away from it—such a mind is in constant revolution. It is an expansive, a creative mind; therefore, like a stone thrown into a pool of still water, its action produces waves, and those waves will form a different civilization altogether.

Questioner: Why do I hate myself when I don't study?

KRISHNAMURTI: Listen to the question. Why do I hate myself when I don't study as I am supposed to? Why do I hate myself when I am not nice, as I should be? In other words, why don't I live up to my ideals?

Now, would it not be much simpler not to have ideals at all? If you had no ideals, would you then have any reason to hate yourself? So why do you say, "I must be kind, I must be generous, I must pay attention, I must study"? If you can find out why, and be free of ideals, then perhaps you will act quite differently—which I shall presently go into.

So, why do you have ideals? First of all, because people have always told you that if you don't have ideals you are a worthless boy. Society, whether it is according to the communist pattern or the capitalist pattern, says, "This is the ideal", and you accept it, you try to live up to it, do you not? Now, before you try to live up to any ideal, should you not find out whether it is necessary to have ideals at all? Surely, that would make far more sense. You have the ideal of Rama and Sita, and so many other ideals which society has given you or which you have invented for yourself. Do you know why you have them? Because you are afraid to be what you are.

Let us keep it simple, don't let us complicate it. You are afraid to be what you are—which means that you have no confidence in yourself. That is why you try to be what society, what your parents and your religion tell you that you should be.

Now, why are you afraid to be what you are? Why don't you start with what you are and not with what you should be? Without understanding what you are, merely to try to change it into what you think you should be has no meaning. Therefore scrap all ideals. I know the older people won't like this, but it doesn't matter. Scrap all ideals, drown them in the river, throw them into the waste-paper basket, and start with what you are—which is what?

You are lazy, you don't want to study, you want to play games, you want to have a good time, like all young people. Start with that. Use your mind to examine what you mean when you talk about having a good time—find out what is actually involved in it, don't go by what your parents or your ideals say. Use your mind to discover why you don't want to study. Use your mind to find out what you want to do in life—what *you* want to do, not what society or some ideal tells you to do. If you give your whole being to this inquiry, then you are a revolutionary; then you have the confidence to create, to be what you are, and in that there is an ever-renewing vitality. But the other way you are dissipating your energy in trying to be like somebody else.

Don't you see, it is really an extraordinary thing that you are so afraid to be what you are; because beauty lies in being what you are. If you see that you are lazy, that you are stupid, and if you understand laziness and come face to face with stupidity without trying to change it into something else, then in that state you will find there is an enormous release, there is great beauty, great intelligence.

Questioner: Even if we do create a new society by revolting against the present one, isn't this creation of a new society still another form of ambition?

KRISHNAMURTI: I am afraid you did not listen to what I said. When the mind revolts within the pattern of society, such a revolt is like a mutiny in a prison, and it is merely another form of ambition. But when the mind understands this whole destructive process of the present society and steps out of it, then its action is not ambitious. Such action may create a new culture, a better social order, a different world, but the mind is not concerned with that creation. Its only concern is to discover what is true; and it is the movement of truth that creates a new world, not the mind which is in revolt against society.

19

Knowledge and Tradition

I wonder how many of you noticed the rainbow last evening? It was just over the water, and one came upon it suddenly. It was a beautiful thing to behold, and it gave one a great sense of joy, an awareness of the vastness and beauty of the earth. To communicate such joy one must have a knowledge of words, the rhythm and beauty of right language, mustn't one? But what is far more important is the feeling itself, the ecstasy that comes with the deep appreciation of something lovely; and this feeling cannot be awakened through the mere cultivation of knowledge or memory.

You see, we must have knowledge to communicate, to tell each other about something; and to cultivate knowledge there must be memory. Without knowledge you cannot fly an airplane, you cannot build a bridge or a lovely house, you cannot construct great roads, look after trees, care for animals and do the many other things that a civilized man must do. To generate electricity, to work in the various sciences, to help man through medicine, and so on—for all this you must have knowledge, information, memory, and in these matters it is necessary to receive the best possible instruction. That is why it is very important that you should have technically first-class teachers to give you right information and help you to cultivate a thorough knowledge of various subjects.

But, you see, while knowledge is necessary at one level, at another level it becomes a hindrance. There is a great deal of knowledge available about physical existence, and it is being added to, all the time. It is essential to have such knowledge and to utilize it for the benefit of man. But is there not another kind of knowledge which, at the psychological level, becomes a hindrance to the discovery of what is true? After all, knowledge is a form of tradition, is it not? And tradition is the cultivation of memory. Tradition in mechanical affairs is essential, but when tradition is used as a means of guiding man inwardly, it becomes a hindrance to the discovery of greater things.

We rely on knowledge, on memory in mechanical things and in our everyday living. Without knowledge we would not be able to drive a car, we would be incapable of doing many things. But knowledge is a hindrance when it becomes a tradition, a belief which guides the mind, the psyche, the inward being; and it also divides people. Have you noticed how people all over the world are divided into groups, calling themselves Hindus, Moslems, Buddhists, Christians, and so on? What divides them? Not the investigations of science, not the knowledge of agriculture, of how to build bridges or fly jet planes. What divides people is tradition, beliefs which condition the mind in a certain way.

So knowledge is a hindrance when it has become a tradition which shapes or conditions the mind to a particular pattern, because then it not only divides people and creates enmity between them, but it also prevents the deep discovery of what is truth, what is life, what is God. To discover what is God, the mind must be free of all tradition, of all accumulation, of all knowledge which it uses as a psychological safeguard.

The function of education is to give the student abundant knowledge in the various fields of human endeavour and at the same time to free his mind from all tradition so that he is able to investigate, to find out, to discover. Otherwise the mind becomes mechanical, burdened with the machinery of knowledge. Unless it is constantly freeing itself from the accumulations of tradition, the mind is incapable of discovering the Supreme, that which is eternal; but it must obviously acquire expanding knowledge and information so that it is capable of dealing with the things that man needs and must produce.

So knowledge, which is the cultivation of memory, is useful and necessary at a certain level, but at another level it becomes a detriment. To recognize the distinction—to see where knowledge is destructive and has to be put aside, and where it is essential and to be allowed to function with as much amplitude as possible—is the beginning of intelligence.

Now, what is happening in education at the present time? You are being given various kinds of knowledge, are you not? When you go to college you may become an engineer, a doctor, or a lawyer, you may take a Ph.D. in mathematics or in some other branch of knowledge, you may study domestic science and learn how to keep house, how to cook, and so on; but nobody helps you to be free of all traditions so that from the very beginning your mind is fresh, eager and therefore capable of discovering something totally new all the time. The philosophies, theories and beliefs which you acquire from books, and which become your tradition, are really a hindrance to the mind, because the mind uses these things as a means of its own psychological security and is therefore conditioned by them. So it is necessary both to free the mind from all tradition, and at the same time to cultivate knowledge, technique; and this is the function of education.

The difficulty is to free the mind from the known so that it can discover what is new all the time. A great mathematician once told of how he had been working on a problem for a number of days and could not find the solution. One morning, as he was taking a walk as usual, he suddenly saw the answer. What had happened? His mind, being quiet, was free to look at the problem, and the problem itself revealed the answer. One must have information about a problem, but the mind must be free of that information to find the answer.

Most of us learn facts, gather information or knowledge, but the mind never learns how to be quiet, how to be free from all the turmoils of life, from the soil in which problems take root. We join societies, adhere to some philosophy, give ourselves over to a belief, but all this is utterly useless because it does not solve our human problems. On the contrary, it brings greater misery, greater sorrow. What is needed is not philosophy or belief, but for the mind to be free to investigate, to discover and to be creative.

You cram up to pass examinations, you gather a lot of information and write it all out to get a degree, hoping to find a job and get married; and is that all? You have acquired knowledge, technique, but your mind is not free, so you become a slave to the existing system—which really means that you are not a creative human being. You may have children, you may paint a few pictures or write an occasional poem, but surely that is not creativeness. There must first be freedom of the mind for creativeness to take place, and then technique can be used to express that creativeness. But to have the technique is meaningless without a creative mind, without the extraordinary creativeness which comes with the discovery of what is true. Unfortunately most of us do not know this creativeness because we have burdened our minds with knowledge, tradition, memory, with what Shankara, Buddha, Marx or some other person has said. Whereas, if your mind is free to discover what is true, then you will find that there comes an abundant and incorruptible richness in which there is great joy. Then all one's relationships—with people, with ideas and with things—have quite a different meaning.

Questioner: Will the naughty boy change through punishment or through love?

KRISHNAMURTI: What do *you* think? Listen very carefully to the question; think it out, feel it out. Will a naughty boy change through punishment or through love? If he changes through punishment, which is a form of compulsion, is that change? You are a bigger person, you have authority as the teacher or the parent, and if you threaten him, frighten him, the poor chap may do as you say; but is that change? Is there change through any form of compulsion? Can there ever be change through legislation, through any form of fear?

And, when you ask if love will bring about a change in the naughty boy, what do you mean by that word 'love'? If to love is to understand the boy—not to change him, but to understand the causes that are producing naughtiness—then that very understanding will bring about in him the cessation of naughtiness. If I want to change the boy so that he will stop being naughty, my very desire to change him is a form of compulsion, is it not? But if I begin to understand why he is naughty, if I can discover and eradicate the causes that are producing naughtiness in him—it may be wrong food, a lack of sleep, want of affection, the fact that he is being teased by another boy, and so on—then the boy will not be naughty. But if my desire is merely to change the boy, which is wanting him to fit into a particular pattern, then I cannot understand him.

You see, this brings up the problem of what we mean by change. Even if the boy ceases to be naughty because of your love for him, which is a kind of influence, is that a real change? It may be love, but it is still a form of pressure on him to do or be something. And when you say a boy must change, what do you mean by that? Change from what to what? From what he is to what he *should* be? If he changes to what he should be, has he not merely modified what he was, and therefore it is no change at all?

To put it differently, if I am greedy and I become non-greedy because you and society and the sacred books all tell me that I must do so, have I changed, or am I merely calling greed by a different name? Whereas, if I am capable of investigating and understanding the whole problem of my greed, then I shall be free of it—which is entirely different from becoming non-greedy.

Questioner: How is one to become intelligent?

KRISHNAMURTI: The moment you try to become intelligent, you cease to be intelligent. This is really important, so give your mind to it a little bit. If I am stupid and everybody tells me that I must become intelligent, what generally happens? I struggle to become intelligent, I study more, I try to get better marks. Then people say, "He is working harder," and pat me on the back; but I continue to be stupid because I have only acquired the trimmings of intelligence. So the problem is, not how to become intelligent, but how to be free of stupidity. If, being stupid, I try to become intelligent, I am still functioning stupidly.

You see, the basic problem is that of change. When you ask, "What is intelligence and how is one to become intelligent?" it implies a concept of what intelligence is, and then you try to become like that concept. Now, to have a formula, a theory or concept of what intelligence is, and to try to mould yourself according to that pattern, is foolish, is it not? Whereas, if one is dull and begins to find out what dullness is without any desire to change it into something else, without saying, "I am dull, stupid, how terrible!", then one will find that in unravelling the problem there comes an intelligence freed of stupidity, and without effort.

Questioner: I am a Moslem. If I don't follow daily the traditions of my religion, my parents threaten to turn me out of the house. What should I do?

KRISHNAMURTI: You who are not Moslems will probably advise the questioner to leave home, will you not? But regardless of the label you wear—Hindu, Parsi, communist, Christian, or what you will—the same thing applies to you, so don't feel superior and ride the high horse. If you tell your parents that their traditions are really old superstitions, *they* also may turn you out of the house.

Now, if you were raised in a particular religion and your father says that you must leave home unless you observe certain practices which you now see to be old superstitions, what are you going to do? It depends on how vitally you don't want to follow the old superstitions, does it not? Will you say, "I have thought about the matter a great deal, and I think that to call oneself a Moslem, a Hindu, a Buddhist, a Christian, or any of these things, is nonsense. If for this reason I must leave home, I will. I am ready to face whatever life brings, even misery and death, because this is what I feel to be right and I am going to stand by it"—will you say that? If you don't, you will just be swallowed by tradition, by the collective.

So, what are you going to do? If education does not give you that kind of confidence, then what is the purpose of education? Is it merely to prepare you to get a job and fit into a society which is obviously destructive? Don't say, "Only a few can break away, and I am not strong enough". Anyone can break away who puts his mind to it. To understand and withstand the pressure of tradition you must have, not strength, but confidence—the tremendous confidence which comes when you know how to think things out for yourself. But you see, your education does not teach you *how* to think; it tells you *what* to think. You are told that you are a Moslem, a Hindu, a Christian, this or that. But it is the function of right education to help you to think for yourself, so that out of your own thinking you feel immense confidence. Then you are a creative human being and not a slavish machine.

Questioner: You tell us that there should be no resistance in paying attention. How can this be?

KRISHNAMURTI: I have said that any form of resistance is inattention, distraction. Don't accept it, think it over. Don't accept anything, it does not matter who says it, but investigate the matter for yourself. If you merely accept, you become mechanical, dull, you are already dead; but if you investigate, if you think things out for yourself, then you are alive, vital, a creative human being.

Now, can you pay attention to what is being said and at the same time be aware that somebody is coming in, without turning your head to see who it is and without any resistance against turning you head? If you resist turning your head to look, your attention has already gone and you are wasting your mental energy in that resistance. So, can there be a state of total attention in which there is no distraction and therefore no resistance? That is, can you pay attention to something with your whole being and yet keep the outside of your consciousness sensitive to all that is happening about you and within yourself?

You see, the mind is an extraordinary instrument, it is constantly absorbing—seeing various forms and colours, receiving innumerable impressions, catching the meaning of words, the significance of a glance, and so on; and our problem is to pay attention to something while at the same time keeping the mind really sensitive to everything that is going on, including all the unconscious impressions and responses.

What I am saying really involves the whole problem of meditation. We cannot enter into that now; but if one doesn't know how to meditate, one is not a mature human being. Meditation is one of the most important things in life—far more important than passing examinations to get a degree. To understand what is right meditation is not to practise meditation. The "practice" of anything in spiritual matters is deadly. To understand what is right meditation there must be an awareness of the operations of one's own consciousness, and then there is complete attention. But complete attention is not possible when there is any form of resistance. You see, most of us are educated to pay attention through resistance, and so our attention is always partial, never complete—and that is why learning becomes tedious, boring, a fearful thing. Therefore it is very important to pay attention in the deep sense of the word, which is to be aware of the workings of one's own mind. Without self-knowledge you cannot pay complete attention. That is why, in a real school, the student must not only be taught various subjects but also helped to be aware of the process of his own thinking. In understanding himself he will know what it is to pay attention without resistance, for the understanding of oneself is the way of meditation.

Questioner: Why are we interested in asking questions?

KRISHNAMURTI: Very simple: because one is curious. Don't you want to know how to play cricket or football, or how to fly a kite? The moment you stop asking questions you are already dead—which is generally what has happened to older people. They have ceased to inquire because their minds are burdened with information, with what others have said; they have accepted and are fixed in tradition. As long as you ask questions you are breaking through, but the moment you begin to accept, you are psychologically dead. So right through life don't accept a thing, but inquire, investigate. Then you will find that your mind is something really extraordinary, it has no end, and to such a mind there is no death.

20

To Be Religious Is to Be Sensitive to Reality

That green field with mustard-yellow flowers and a stream running through it is a lovely thing to look upon, is it not? Yesterday evening I was watching it, and in seeing the extraordinary beauty and quietness of the countryside one invariably asks oneself what is beauty. There is an immediate response to that which is lovely and also to that which is ugly, the response of pleasure or of pain, and we put that feeling into words saying, "This is beautiful" or "This is ugly." But what matters is not the pleasure or the pain; rather, it is to be in communion with everything, to be sensitive both to the ugly and the beautiful.

Now, what is beauty? This is one of the most fundamental questions, it is not superficial, so don't brush it aside. To understand what beauty is, to have that sense of goodness which comes when the mind and heart are in communion with something lovely without any hindrance so that one feels completely at ease—surely, this has great significance in life; and until we know this response to beauty our lives will be very shallow. One may be surrounded by great beauty, by mountains and fields and rivers, but unless one is alive to it all one might just as well be dead.

You girls and boys and older people just put to yourselves this question: what is beauty? Cleanliness, tidiness of dress, a smile, a graceful gesture, the rhythm of walking, a flower in your hair, good manners, clarity of speech, thoughtfulness, being considerate of others, which includes punctuality—all this is part of beauty; but it is only on the surface, is it not? And is that all there is to beauty, or is there something much deeper?

There is beauty of form, beauty of design, beauty of life. Have you observed the lovely shape of a tree when it is in full foliage, or the extraordinary delicacy of a tree naked against the sky? Such things are beautiful to behold, but they are all the superficial expressions of something much deeper. So what is it that we call beauty?

You may have a beautiful face, clean-cut features, you may dress with good taste and have polished manners, you may paint well or write about the beauty of the landscape, but without this inward sense of goodness all the external appurtenances of beauty lead to a very superficial, sophisticated life, a life without much significance.

So we must find out what beauty really is, must we not? Mind you, I am not saying that we should avoid the outward expressions of beauty. We must all have good manners, we must be physically clean and dress tastefully, without ostentation, we must be punctual, clear in our speech, and all the rest of it. These things are necessary and they create a pleasant atmosphere; but by themselves they have not much significance.

It is inward beauty that gives grace, an exquisite gentleness to outward form and movement. And what is this inward beauty without which one's life is very shallow? Have you ever thought about it? Probably not. You are too busy, your minds are too occupied with study, with play, with talking, laughing and teasing each other. But to help you to discover what is inward beauty, without which outward form and movement have very little meaning, is one of the functions of right education; and the deep appreciation of beauty is an essential part of your own life.

Can a shallow mind appreciate beauty? It may talk about beauty; but can it experience this welling up of immense joy upon looking at something that is really lovely? When the mind is merely concerned with itself and its own activities, it is not beautiful; whatever it does, it remains ugly, limited, therefore it is incapable of knowing what beauty is. Whereas, a mind that is not concerned with itself, that is free of ambition, a mind that is not caught up in its own desires or driven by its own pursuit of success—such a mind is not shallow, and it flowers in goodness. Do you understand? It is this inward goodness that gives beauty, even to a so-called ugly face. When there is inward goodness, the ugly face is transformed, for inward goodness is really a deeply religious feeling.

Do you know what it is to be religious? It has nothing to do with temple bells, though they sound nice in the distance, nor with *pujas*, nor with the ceremonies of the priests and all the rest of the ritualistic nonsense. To be religious is to be sensitive to reality. Your total being—body, mind and heart—is sensitive to beauty and to ugliness, to the donkey tied to a post, to the poverty and filth in this town, to laughter and tears, to everything about you. From this sensitivity for the whole of existence springs goodness, love; and without this sensitivity there is no beauty, though you may have talent, be very well dressed, ride in an expensive car and be scrupulously clean.

Love is something extraordinary, is it not? You cannot love if you are thinking about yourself—which does not mean that you must think about somebody else. Love *is*, it has no object. The mind that loves is really a religious mind because it is in the movement of reality, of truth, of God, and it is only such a mind that can know what beauty is. The mind that is not caught in any philosophy, that is not enclosed in any system or belief, that is not driven by its own ambition and is therefore sensitive, alert, watchful—such a mind has beauty.

It is very important while you are young to learn to be tidy and clean, to sit well without restless movement, to have good table manners and to be considerate, punctual; but all these things, however necessary, are superficial, and if you merely cultivate the superficial without understanding the deeper thing, you will never know the real significance of beauty. A mind that does not belong to any nation, group or society, that has no authority, that is not motivated by ambition or held by fear—such a mind is always flowering in love and goodness. Because it is in the movement of reality, it knows what beauty is; being sensitive to both the ugly and the beautiful, it is a creative mind, it has limitless understanding.

Questioner: If I have ambition in childhood, will I be able to fulfil it as I grow up?

KRISHNAMURTI: A childhood ambition is generally not very enduring, is it? A little boy wants to be an engine driver; or he sees a jet plane go flashing across the sky and he wants to be a pilot; or he hears some political orator and wants to be like him, or sees a *sannyasi* and decides to become one too. A girl may want to have many children, or be the wife of a rich man and live in a big house, or she may aspire to paint or to write poems.

Now, will childhood dreams be fulfilled? And are dreams worth fulfilling? To seek the fulfilment of any desire, no matter what it is, always brings sorrow. Perhaps you have not yet noticed this, but you will as you grow up. Sorrow is the shadow of desire. If I want to be rich or famous, I struggle to reach my goal, pushing others aside and creating enmity; and, even though I may get what I want, sooner or later something invariably happens. I fall ill, or in the very fulfilling of my desire I long for something more; and there is always death lurking around the corner. Ambition, desire and fulfilment lead inevitably to frustration, sorrow. You can watch this process for yourself. Study the older people around you, the men who are famous, who are great in the land, those who have made names for themselves and have power. Look at their faces; see how sad, or how fat and pompous they are. Their faces have ugly lines. They don't flower in goodness because in their hearts there is sorrow.

Is it not possible to live in this world without ambition, just being what you are? If you begin to understand what you are without trying to change it, then what you are undergoes a transformation. I think one can live in this world anonymously, completely unknown, without being famous, ambitious, cruel. One can live very happily when no importance is given to the self; and this also is part of right education.

The whole world is worshipping success. You hear stories of how the poor boy studied at night and eventually became a judge, or how he began by selling newspapers and ended up a multi-millionaire. You are fed on the glorification of success. With the achievement of great success there is also great sorrow; but most of us are caught up in the desire to achieve, and success is much more important to us than the understanding and dissolution of sorrow.

Questioner: In the present social system is it not very difficult to put into action what you are talking about?

KRISHNAMURTI: When you feel very strongly about something, do you consider it difficult to put it into action? When you are keen to play cricket, you play it with your whole being, don't you? And do you call it difficult? It is only when you don't vitally feel the truth of something that you say it is difficult to put it into action. You don't love it. That which you love you do with ardour, there is joy in it, and then what society or what your parents may say does not matter. But if you are not deeply convinced, if you do not feel free and happy in doing what you think is right, surely your interest in it is false, unreal; therefore it becomes mountainous and you say it is difficult to put it into action.

In doing what you love to do there will of course be difficulties, but that won't matter to you, it is part of life. You see, we have made a philosophy of difficulty, we consider it a virtue to make effort, to struggle, to oppose.

I am not talking of proficiency through effort and struggle, but of the love of doing something. But don't battle against society, don't tackle dead tradition, unless you have this love in you, for your struggle will be meaningless, and you will merely create more mischief. Whereas, if you deeply feel what is right and can therefore stand alone, then your action born of love will have extraordinary significance, it will have vitality, beauty.

You know, it is only in a very quiet mind that great things are born; and a quiet mind does not come about through effort, through control, through discipline.

Questioner: What do you mean by a total change, and how can it be realized in one's own being?

KRISHNAMURTI: Do you think there can be a total change if you try to bring it about? Do you know what change is? Suppose you are ambitious and you have begun to see all that is involved in ambition: hope, satisfaction, frustration, cruelty, sorrow, inconsideration, greed, envy, an utter lack of love. Seeing all this, what are you to do? To make an effort to change or transform ambition is another form of ambition, is it not? It implies a desire to be something else. You may reject one desire, but in that very process you cultivate another desire which also brings sorrow.

Now, if you see that ambition brings sorrow, and that the desire to put an end to ambition also brings sorrow, if you see the truth of this very clearly for yourself and do not act, but allow the truth to act, then that truth brings about a fundamental change in the mind, a total revolution. But this requires a great deal of attention, penetration, insight.

When you are told, as you all are, that you should be good, that you should love, what generally happens? You say, "I must practise being good, I must show love to my parents, to the servant, to the donkey, to everything." That means you are making an effort to show love —and then "love" becomes very shoddy, very pretty, as it does with those nationalistic people who are everlastingly practising brotherhood, which is silly, stupid. It is greed that causes these practices. But if you see the truth of nationalism, of greed, and let that truth work upon you, let that truth act, then you will be brotherly without making any effort. A mind that practises love cannot love. But if you love and do not interfere with it, then love will operate.

Questioner: Sir, what is self-expansion?

KRISHNAMURTI: If you want to become the governor or a famous professor, if you imitate some big man or hero, if you try to follow your *guru* or a saint, then that process of becoming, imitating, following is a form of self-expansion, is it not? An ambitious man, a man who wants to be great, who wants to fulfil himself may say, "I am doing this in the name of peace and for the sake of my country"; but his action is still the expansion of himself.

Questioner: Why is the rich man proud?

KRISHNAMURTI: A little boy asks why the rich man is proud. Have you really noticed that the rich man is proud? And do not the poor also have pride? We all have our own peculiar arrogance which we show in different ways. The rich man, the poor man, the learned man, the man of capacity, the saint, the leader—each in his own way has the feeling that he has arrived, that he is a success, that he is somebody or can do something. But the man who is nobody, who does not want to be a somebody, who is just himself and understands himself—such a man is free of arrogance, of pride.

Questioner: Why are we always caught in the "me" and the "mine", and why do we keep bringing up in our meetings with you the problems which this state of mind produces?

Krishnamurti: Do you really want to know, or has somebody prompted you to ask this question? The problem of the "me" and the "mine" is one in which we are all involved. It is really the only problem we have, and we are everlastingly talking about it in different ways, sometimes in terms of fulfilment and sometimes in terms of frustration, sorrow. The desire to have lasting happiness, the fear of dying or of losing property, the pleasure of being flattered, the resentment of being insulted, the quarrelling over your god and my god, your way and my way—the mind is ceaselessly occupied with all this and nothing else. It may pretend to seek peace, to feel brotherly, to be good, to love, but behind this screen of words it continues to be caught up in the conflict of the "me" and the "mine", and that is why it creates the problems which you bring up every morning in different words.

Questioner: Why do women dress themselves up?

Krishnamurti: Have you not asked them? And have you never watched the birds? Often it is the male bird that has more colour, more sprightliness. To be physically attractive is part of the sexual relationship to produce young. That is life. And the boys also do it. As they grow up they like to comb their hair in a particular way, wear a nice cap, put on attractive clothes—which is the same thing. We all want to show off. The rich man in his expensive car, the girl who makes herself more beautiful, the boy who tries to be very smart—they all want to show that they have something. It is a strange world, is it not? You see, a lily or a rose never pretends, and its beauty is that it is what it is.

21

The Purpose of Learning

Are you interested in trying to find out what is learning? You go to school to learn, don't you? And what is learning? Have you ever thought about it? How do you learn, why do you learn, and what is it that you are learning? What is the meaning, the deeper significance of learning? You have to learn to read and write, to study various subjects, and also to acquire a technique, to prepare yourself for a profession by which to earn a livelihood. We mean all of that when we talk about learning—and then most of us stop there. As soon as we pass certain examinations and have a job, a profession, we seem to forget all about learning.

But is there an end to learning? We say that learning from books and learning from experience are two different things; and are they? From books we learn that other people have written about sciences, for example. Then we make our own expeirments and continue to learn through those experiments. And we also learn through experience—at least that is what we say. But after all, to fathom the extraordinary depths of life, to find out what God or truth is, there must be freedom; and, through experience, is there freedom to find out, to learn?

Have you thought about what experience is? It is the feeling in reponse to a challenge, is it not? To respond to a challenge is experience. And do you learn through experience? When you respond to a challenge, to a stimulus, your response is based on your conditioning, on the education you have received, on your cultural, religious, social and economic background. You respond to a challenge conditioned by your background as a Hindu, a Christian, a communist, or whatever you are. If you do not break away from your background, your response to any challenge only strengthens or modifies that background. Hence you are really never free to explore, to discover, to understand what is truth, what is God.

So, experience does not free the mind, and learning through experience is only a process of forming new patterns based on one's old conditioning. I think it is very important to understand this, because as we grow older we get more and more entrenched in our experience, hoping thereby to learn; but what we learn is dictated by the background, which means that through the experience by which we learn there is never freedom but only the modification of conditioning.

Now, what is learning? You begin by learning how to read and write, how to sit quietly, how to obey or not to obey; you learn the history of this or that country, you learn languages which are necessary for communication; you learn how to earn a livelihood, how to enrich the fields, and so on. But is there a state of learning in which the mind is free of the background, a state in which there is no search? Do you understand the question?

What we call learning is a continuous process of adjusting, resisting, subjugating; we learn either to avoid or to gain something. Now, is there a state in which the mind is not the instrument of learning but of being? Do you see the difference? As long as we are acquiring, getting, avoiding, the mind must learn, and in such learning there is always a great deal of tension, resistance. To learn you must concentrate, must you not? And what is concentration?

Have you ever noticed what happens when you concentrate on something? When you are required to study a book which you don't want to study, or even if you do want to study, you have to resist and put aside other things. You resist the inclination to look out of the window, or to talk to somebody, in order to concentrate. So in concentration there is always effort, is there not? In concentration there is a motive, an incentive, an effort to learn in order to acquire something; and our life is a series of such efforts, a state of tension in which we are trying to learn. But if there is no tension at all, no acquiring, no laying up of knowledge, is not the mind then capable of learning much more deeply and swiftly? Then it becomes an instrument of inquiry to find out what is truth, what is beauty, what is God—which means, really, that it does not submit to any authority, whether it be the authority of knowledge or society, of religion, culture or conditioning.

You see, it is only when the mind is free from the burden of knowledge that it can find out what is true; and in the process of finding out, there is no accumulation, is there? The moment you begin to accumulate what you have experienced or learnt, it becomes an anchorage which holds your mind and prevents it from going further. In the process of inquiry the mind sheds from day to day what it has learnt so that it is always fresh, uncontaminated by yesterday's experience. Truth is living, it is not static, and the mind that would discover truth must also be living, not burdened with knowledge or experience. Then only is there that state in which truth can come into being.

All this may be difficult in the verbal sense, but the meaning is not difficult if you apply your mind to it. To inquire into the deeper things of life, the mind must be free; but the moment you learn and make that learning the basis of further inquiry, your mind is not free and you are no longer inquiring.

Questioner: Why do we so easily forget what we find difficult to learn?

KRISHNAMURTI: Are you learning merely because circumstances force you to learn? After all, if you are studying physics and mathematics you really want to become a lawyer, you soon forget the physics and mathematics. Do you really learn if you have an incentive to learn? If you want to pass certain examinations merely in order to find a job and get married, you may make an effort to concentrate, to learn; but once you pass the examinations you soon forget what you have learned, do you not? When learning is only a means to get somewhere, the moment you have got where you want to go, you forget the means—and surely that is not learning at all. So there may be the state of learning only when there is no motive, no incentive, when you do the thing for the love of itself.

Questioner: What is the significance of the word "progress"?

KRISHNAMURTI: Like most people, you have ideals, have you not? And the ideal is not real, not factual; it is what *should* be, it is something in the future. Now, what I say is this: forget the ideal, and be aware of what you are. Do not pursue what *should* be, but understand what *is*. The understanding of what you actually are is far more important than the pursuit of what you *should* be.

Why? Because in understanding what you are there begins a spontaneous process of transformation, whereas in becoming what you think you *should* be there is no change at all, but only a continuation of the same old thing in a different form. If the mind, seeing that it is stupid, tries to change its stupidity into intelligence, which is what *should* be, that is silly, it has no meaning, no reality; it is only the pursuit of a self-projection, a postponement of the understanding of what is. As long as the mind tries to change its stupidity into something else, it remains stupid. But if the mind says, "I realize that I am stupid and I want to understand what stupidity is, therefore I shall go into it, I shall observe how it comes into being", then that very process of inquiry brings about a fundamental transformation.

"What is the significance of the word 'progress'?" *Is* there such a thing as progress? You see the bullock cart moving at two miles an hour, and that extraordinary thing called the jet plane travelling at 600 or more miles per hour. That is progress, is it not? There is technological progress: better means of communication, better health and so on. But is there any other form of progress? Is there psychological progress in the sense of spiritual advancement through time? Is the idea of progress in spirituality really spiritual, or merely an invention of the mind?

You know, it is very important to ask fundamental questions; but unfortunately we find very easy answers to fundamental questions. We think the easy answer is a solution, but it is not. We must ask a fundamental question and let that question operate, let it work in us to find out what is the truth of it.

Progress implies time, does it not? After all, it has taken us centuries to come from the bullock cart to the jet plane. Now, we think that we can find reality or God in the same way, through time. We are here, and we think of God as being over there, or somewhere far away, and to cover that distance, that intervening space, we say we need time. But God or reality is not fixed, and neither are we fixed; there is no fixed point from which to start and no fixed point towards which to move. For reasons of psychological security we cling to the idea that there is a fixed point in each of us, and that reality is also fixed; but this is an illusion, it is not true. The moment we want time in which to evolve or progress inwardly, spiritually, what we are doing is no longer spiritual, because truth is not of time. A mind which is caught up in time demands time to find reality. But reality is beyond time, it has no fixed point. The mind must be free of all its accumulations, conscious as well as unconscious, and only then is it capable of finding out what is truth, what is God.

Questioner: Why do birds fly away when I come near?

KRISHNAMURTI: How nice it would be if the birds did not fly away when you came near! If you could touch them, be friendly with them, how lovely it would be! But you see, we human beings are cruel people. We kill the birds, torture them, we catch them in nets and put them in cages. Think of a lovely parrot in a cage! Every evening it calls to its mate and sees the other birds flying across the open sky. When we do all these things to the birds, do you think they will not be frightened when we come near them? But if you sit quietly in an isolated spot and are very still, really gentle, you will soon find that the birds come to you; they hover quite close and you can observe their alert movements, their delicate claws, the extraordinary strength and beauty of their feathers. But to do that you must have immense patience, which means you must have a great deal of love, and also there must be no fear. Animals seem to sense fear in us, and they in turn get frightened and run away. That is why it is very important to understand oneself.

You try sitting very still under a tree, but not just for two or three minutes, because the birds won't get used to you in so short a time. Go and sit quietly under the same tree every day, and you will soon begin to be aware that everything around you is living. You will see the blades of grass sparkling in the sunshine, the ceaseless activity of the little birds, the extraordinary sheen of a snake, or a kite flying high in the skies enjoying the breeze without a movement of its wings. But to see all this and to feel the joy of it you must have real quietness inside you.

Questioner: What is the difference between you and me?

KRISHNAMURTI: Is there any fundamental difference between us? You may have a fair skin and I may be quite dark; you may be very clever and know a lot more than I; or I may live in a village while you travel all over the world, and so on. Obviously there are differences in form, in speech, in knowledge, in manners, in tradition and culture; but whether we are Brahmins or non-Brahmins, whether we are Americans, Russians, Japanese, Chinese, or what you will, is there not a great similarity between us all? We are all afraid, we all want security, we all want to be loved, we all want to eat and to be happy. But you see, the superficial differences destroy our awareness of the fundamental similarity between us as human beings. To understand and to be free of that similarity brings about great love, great thoughtfulness. Unfortunately, most of us are caught up in, and therefore divided by, the superficial differences of race, of culture, of belief. Beliefs are a curse, they divide people and create anatagonism. It is only by going beyond all beliefs, beyond all differences and similarities, that the mind can be free to find out what is true.

Questioner: Why does the teacher get cross with me when I smoke?

KRISHNAMURTI: Probably he has told you many times not to smoke because it is not very good for little boys; but you keep on smoking because you like the taste, so he gets cross with you. Now, what do *you* think? Do you think one should get used to smoking, or acquire any other habit, while one is so very young? If at your age your body gets accustomed to smoking, it means you are already a slave to something; and is that not a terrible thing? Smoking may be all right for older people, but even that is extremely doubtful. Unfortunately, they have their excuses for being slaves to various habits. But you who are very young, immature, adolescent, you who are still growing—why should you get used to anything, or fall into any habit, which only makes you insensitive? The moment the mind gets used to something it begins to function in the groove of habit, therefore it becomes dull, it is no longer vulnerable; it loses that sensibility which is necessary to find out what is God, what is beauty, what is love.

Questioner: Why do men hunt tigers?

KRISHNAMURTI: Because they want to kill for the excitement of killing. We all do lots of thoughtless things —like tearing the wings from a fly to see what will happen. We gossip and say harsh things about others; we kill to eat; we kill for so-called peace; we kill for our country or for our ideas. So there is a great streak of cruelty in us, is there not? But if one can understand and put that aside, then it is great fun just to watch the tiger go by—as several of us did one evening near Bombay. A friend took us into the forest in his car to look for a tiger which somebody had seen nearby. We were returning and had just rounded a curve, when suddenly there was the tiger in the middle of the road. Yellow and black, sleek and lean, with a long tail, he was a lovely thing to watch, full of grace and power. We switched off the headlights and he came growling towards us, passing so close that he almost touched the car. It was a marvellous sight. If one can watch a thing like that without a gun it is much more fun, and there is great beauty in it.

Questioner: Why are we burdened with sorrow?

KRISHNAMURTI: We accept sorrow as an inevitable part of life and we build philosophies around it; we justify sorrow, and we say that sorrow is necessary in order to find God. I say, on the contrary, there is sorrow because man is cruel to man. Also we don't understand a great many things in life which therefore bring sorrow—things like death, like not having a job, like seeing the poor in their misery. We don't understand all this, so we are tortured; and the more sensitive one is, the more one suffers. Instead of understanding these things, we justify sorrow; instead of revolting against this whole rotten system and breaking through it, we merely adjust ourselves to it. To be free of sorrow one must be free of the desire to do harm—and also of the desire to do "good", the so-called good that is equally the result of our conditioning.

22

The Simplicity of Love

A man in *sannyasi* robes used to come every morning to gather flowers from the trees in a nearby garden. His hands and his eyes were greedy for the flowers, and he picked every flower within reach. He was evidently going to offer them to some dead image, a thing made of stone. The flowers were lovely, tender things just opening to the morning sun, and he did not pick them gently, but tore them off, viciously stripping the garden of whatever it held. His god demanded lots of flowers—lots of living things for a dead stone image.

Another day I watched some young boys picking flowers. They were not going to offer the flowers to any god; they were talking and thoughtlessly tearing off the flowers, and throwing them away. Have you ever observed yourself doing this? I wonder why you do it? As you walk along you will break off a twig, strip away the leaves and drop it. Have you not noticed this thoughtless action on your part? The grown-up people do it too, they have their own way of expressing their inner brutality, this appalling disrespect for living things. They talk about harmlessness, yet everything they do is destructive.

One can understand your picking a flower or two to put in your hair, or to give to somebody with love; but why do you just tear at the flowers? The grown-ups are ugly in their ambition, they butcher each other in their wars and corrupt each other with money. They have their own forms of hideous action; and apparently the young people here as elsewhere are following in their footsteps.

The other day I was out walking with one of the boys and we came upon a stone lying on the road. When I removed it, he asked, "Why did you do that?" What does this indicate? Is it not a lack of consideration, respect? You show respect out of fear, do you not? You promptly jump up when an elder comes into the room, but that is not respect, it is fear; because if you really felt respect you would not destroy the flowers, you would remove a stone from the road, you would tend the trees and help to take care of the garden. But, whether we are old or young, we have no real feeling of consideration. Why? Is it that we don't know what love is?

Do you understand what simple love is? Not the complexity of sexual love, nor the love of God, but just love, being tender, really gentle in one's whole approach to all things. At home you don't always get this simple love, your parents are too busy; at home there may be no real affection, no tenderness, so you come here with that background of insensitivity and you behave like everybody else. And how is one to bring about sensitivity? Not that you must have regulations against picking the flowers; for when you are merely restrained by regulations, there is fear. But how is there to come into being this sensitivity which makes you alert not to do any harm to people, to animals, to flowers?

Are you interested in all this? You should be. If you are not interested in being sensitive, you might as well be dead—and most people are. Though they eat three meals a day, have jobs, procreate children, drive cars, wear fine clothes, most people are as good as dead.

Do you know what it means to be sensitive? It means, surely, to have a tender feeling for things: to see an animal suffering and do something about it, to remove a stone from the path because so many bare feet walk there, to pick up a nail on the road because somebody's car might get a puncture. To be sensitive is to feel for people, for birds, for flowers, for trees—not because they are yours, but just because you are awake to the extraordinary beauty of things. And how is this sensitivity to be brought about?

The moment you are deeply sensitive you naturally do not pluck the flowers; there is a spontaneous desire not to destroy things, not to hurt people, which means having real respect, love. To love is the most important thing in life. But what do we mean by love? When you love someone because that person loves you in return, surely that is not love. To love is to have that extraordinary feeling of affection without asking anything in return. You may be very clever, you may pass all your examinations, get a doctorate and achieve a high position, but if you have not this sensitivity, this feeling of simple love, your heart will be empty and you will be miserable for the rest of your life.

So it is very important for the heart to be filled with this sense of affection, for then you won't destroy, you won't be ruthless, and there won't be wars any more. Then you will be happy human beings; and because you are happy you won't pray, you won't *seek* God, for that happiness itself is God.

Now, how is this love to come into being? Surely, love must begin with the educator, the teacher. If, besides giving you information about mathematics, geography, or history, the teacher has this feeling of love in his heart and talks about it; if he spontaneously removes the stone from the road and does not allow the servant to do all the dirty jobs; if in his conversation, in his work, in his play, when he eats, when he is with you or by himself, he feels this strange thing and points it out to you often, then you also will know what it is to love.

You may have a clear skin, a nice face, you may wear a lovely *sari* or be a great athlete, but without love in your heart you are an ugly human being, ugly beyond measure; and when you love, whether your face is homely or beautiful, it has a radiance. To love is the greatest thing in life; and it is very important to talk about love, to feel it, to nourish it, to treasure it, otherwise it is soon dissipated, for the world is very brutal. If while you are young you don't feel love, if you don't look with love at people, at animals, at flowers, when you grow up you will find that your life is empty; you will be very lonely, and the dark shadows of fear will follow you always. But the moment you have in your heart this extraordinary thing called love and feel the depth, the delight, the ecstasy of it, you will discover that for you the world is transformed.

Questioner: Why is it that always so many rich and important people are invited to school functions?

KRISHNAMURTI: What do *you* think? Don't you want your father to be an important man? Are you not proud if he becomes a member of parliament and is mentioned in the newspapers? If he takes you to live in a big house, or if he goes to Europe and comes back puffing a cigar, are you not pleased?

You see, the wealthy and those in power are very useful to institutions. The institution flatters them and they do something for the institution, so it works both ways. But the question is not just why the school invites the important people to its functions; it is why you also want to be an important person, or why you want to marry the richest, the best known, or the most handsome man. Don't you all want to be a big something or other? And when you have those desires, you have in you already the seed of corruption. Do you understand what I am saying?

Put aside for the moment the question of why the school invites the wealthy because there are also poor people at these functions. But do any of you sit near the poor people, near the villagers? Do you? And have you noticed another extraordinary thing: how the *sannyasis* want to be seated prominently, how they push their way to the front? We all want to have prominence, recognition. The true Brahmin is one who does not ask anything from anyone, not because he is proud, but because he is a light unto himself; but we have lost all that.

You know, there is a marvellous story about Alexander when he came to India. Having conquered the country, he wanted to meet the prime minister who had created such order in the land and had brought about such honesty, such incorruptibility among the people. When the king explained that the prime minister was a Brahmin who had returned to his village, Alexander asked that he come to see him. The king sent for the prime minister, but he would not come because he did not care to show himself off to anyone. Unfortunately we have lost that spirit. Being in ourselves empty, dull, sorrowful, we are psychological beggars, seeking someone or something to nourish us, to give us hope, to sustain us, and that is why we make normal things ugly.

It is all right for some prominent official to come to lay the cornerstone of a building; what harm is there in that? But what is corrupting is the whole spirit behind it. You never go to visit the villagers, do you? You never talk to them, feel with them, see for yourself how little they have to eat, how endlessly they work day after day without rest; but because I happen to have pointed out to you certain things, you are ready to criticize others. Don't sit around and criticize, that is empty, but go and find out for yourself what the conditions are in the villages and do something there: plant a tree, talk to the villagers, invite them here, play with their children. Then you will find that a different kind of society comes into being, because there will be love in the land. A society without love is like a land without rivers, it is as a desert; but where there are rivers the land is rich, it has abundance, it has beauty. Most of us grow up without love, and that is why we have created a society as hideous as the people who live in it.

Questioner: You say that God is not in the graven image, but others say that he is indeed there, and that if we have faith in our hearts his power will manifest itself. What is the truth of worship?

KRISHNAMURTI: The world is as full of opinions as it is of people. And you know what an opinion is. You say this, and somebody else says that. Each one has an opinion, but opinion is not truth; therefore do not listen to mere opinion, it does not matter *whose* it is, but find out for yourself what is true. Opinion can be changed overnight, but truth cannot be changed.

Now, you want to find out for yourself whether God or truth is in the graven image, do you not? What is a graven image? It is a thing conceived by the mind and fashioned of wood or of stone by the hand. The mind projects the image; and do you think an image projected by the mind is God, though a million people assert that it is?

You say that if the mind has faith in the image, then the image will give power to the mind. Obviously; the mind creates the image and then derives power from its own creation. That is what the mind is everlastingly doing: producing images and drawing strength, happiness, benefit from those images, thereby remaining empty, inwardly poverty-stricken. So what is important is not the image, or what the millions say about it, but to understand the operation of your own mind.

The mind makes and unmakes gods, it can be cruel or kind. The mind has the power to do the most extraordinary things. It can hold opinions, it can create illusions, it can invent jet planes that travel at tremendous speed; it can build beautiful bridges, lay vast railways, devise machines that calculate beyond the capacity of man. But the mind cannot create truth. What it creates is not truth, it is merely an opinion, a judgment. So it is important to find out for yourself what is true.

To find out what is true, the mind must be without any movement, completely still. That stillness is the act of worship—not your going to the temple to offer flowers and pushing aside the beggar on the way. You propitiate the gods because you are afraid of them, but that is not worship. When you understand the mind and the mind is completely still, not *made* still, then that stillness is the act of worship; and in that stillness there comes into being that which is true, that which is beautiful, that which is God.

Questioner: You said one day that we should sit quietly and watch the activity of our own mind; but our thoughts disappear as soon as we begin consciously to observe them. How can we perceive our own mind when the mind is the perceiver as well as that which it perceives?

KRISHNAMURTI: This is a very complex question, and many things are involved in it.

Now, is there a perceiver, or only perception? Please

follow this closely. Is there a thinker, or only thinking? Surely, the thinker does not exist first. First there is thinking, and then thinking creates the thinker—which means that a separation in thinking has taken place. It is when this separation takes place that there comes into being the watcher and the watched, the perceiver and the object of perception. As the questioner says, if you watch your mind, if you observe a thought, that thought disappears, it fades away; but there is actually only perception, not a perceiver. When you look at a flower, when you just see it, at the moment is there an entity who sees? Or is there only seeing? Seeing the flower makes you say, "How nice it is, I want it"; so the "I" comes into being through desire, fear, greed, ambition, which follow in the wake of seeing. It is these that create the "I", and the "I" is non-existent without them.

If you go deeper into this whole question you will discover that when the mind is very quiet, completely still, when there is not a movement of thought and therefore no experiencer, no observer, then that very stillness has its own creative understanding. In that stillness the mind is transformed into something else. But the mind cannot find that stillness through any means, through any discipline, through any practice; it does not come about through sitting in a corner and trying to concentrate. That stillness comes when you understand the ways of the mind. It is the mind that has created the stone image which people worship; it is the mind that has created the *Gita*, the organized religions, the innumerable beliefs; and, to find out what is real, you must go beyond the creations of the mind.

Questioner: Is man only mind and brain, or something more than this?

KRISHNAMURTI: How are you going to find out? If you merely believe, speculate, or accept what Shankara, Buddha, or somebody else has said, you are not investigating, you are not trying to find out what is true.

You have only one instrument, which is the mind; and the mind is the brain also. Therefore, to find out the truth of this matter, you must understand the ways of the mind, must you not? If the mind is crooked you will never see straight; if the mind is very limited you cannot perceive the illimitable. The mind is the instrument of perception and, to perceive truly, the mind must be made straight, it must be cleansed of all conditioning, of all fear. The mind must also be free of knowledge, because knowledge diverts the mind and makes things twisted. The enormous capacity of the mind to invent, to imagine, to speculate, to think—must not this capacity be put aside so that the mind is very clear and very simple? Because it is only the innocent mind, the mind that has experienced vastly and yet is free of knowledge and experience—it is only such a mind that can discover that which is more than brain and mind. Otherwise what you discover will be coloured by what you have already experienced, and your experience is the result of your conditioning.

Questioner: What is the difference between need and greed?

KRISHNAMURTI: Don't you know? Don't you know when you have what you need? And does not something tell you when you are greedy? Begin at the lowest level, and you will see it is so. You know that when you have enough clothes, jewels, or whatever it is, you don't have to philosophize about it. But the moment need moves into the field of greed, it is then that you begin to philosophize, to rationalize, to explain away your greed. A good hospital, for example, requires so many beds, a certain standard of cleanliness, certain antiseptics, this and that. A travelling man must perhaps have a car, an overcoat, and so on. That is need. You need a certain knowledge and skill to carry on your craft. If you are an engineer you must know certain things—but that knowledge can become an instrument of greed. Through greed the mind uses the objects of need as a means of self-advancement. It is a very simple process if you observe it. If, being aware of your actual needs, you also see how greed comes in, how the mind uses the objects of need for its own aggrandizement, then it is not very difficult to distinguish between need and greed.

Questioner: If the mind and the brain are one, then why is it that when a thought or an urge arises which the brain tells us is ugly the mind so often goes on with it?

KRISHNAMURTI: Actually what takes places? If a pin pricks your arm, the nerves carry the sensation to your brain, the brain translates it as pain, then the mind rebels against the pain, and you take away the pin or otherwise do something about it. But there are some things which the mind goes on with, even though it knows them to be ugly or stupid. It knows how essentially stupid it is to smoke, and yet one goes on smoking. Why? Because it likes the sensations of smoking, and that is all. If the mind were as keenly aware of the stupidity of smoking as it is of the pain of a pinprick, it would stop smoking immediately. But it doesn't want to see it that clearly because smoking has become a pleasurable habit. It is the same with greed or violence. If greed were as painful to you as the pinprick in your arm, you would instantly stop being greedy, you wouldn't philosophize about it;

and if you were really awake to the full significance of violence, you wouldn't write volumes about non-violence—which is all nonsense, because you don't feel it, you just talk about it. If you eat something which gives you a violent tummy-ache, you don't go on eating it, do you? You put it aside immediately. Similarly, if you once realized that envy and ambition are poisonous, vicious, cruel, as deadly as the sting of a cobra, you would awaken to them. But, you see, the mind does not want to look at these things too closely; in this area it has vested interests, and it refuses to admit that ambition, envy, greed, lust are poisonous. Therefore it says, "Let us discuss non-greed, non-violence, let us have ideals"—and in the meantime it carries on with its poisons. So find out for yourself how corrupting, how destructive and poisonous these things are, and you will soon drop them; but if you merely say, "I must not" and go on as before, you are playing the hypocrite. Be one thing or the other, hot or cold.

23

The Need to Be Alone

Is it not a very strange thing in this world, where there is so much distraction, entertainment, that almost everybody is a spectator and very few are players? Whenever we have a little free time, most of us seek some form of amusement. We pick up a serious book, a novel, or a magazine. If we are in America we turn on the radio or the television, or we indulge in incessant talk. There is a constant demand to be amused, to be entertained, to be taken away from ourselves. We are afraid to be alone, afraid to be without a companion, without a distraction of some sort. Very few of us ever walk in the fields and the woods, not talking or singing songs, but just walking quietly and observing things about us and within ourselves. We almost never do that because, you see, most of us are very bored; we are caught in a dull routine of learning or teaching, of household duties or a job, and so in our free time we want to be amused, either lightly or seriously. We read, or go to the cinema—or we turn to a religion, which is the same thing. Religion too has become a form of distraction, a kind of serious escape from boredom, from routine.

I don't know if you have noticed all this. Most people are constantly occupied with something—with *puja*, with the repetition of certain words, with worrying over this or that—because they are frightened to be alone with themselves. You try being alone, without any form of distraction, and you will see how quickly you want to get away from yourself and forget what you are. That is why this enormous structure of professional amusement, of automated distraction, is so prominent a part of what we call civilization. If you observe you will see that people the world over are becoming more and more distracted, increasingly sophisticated and worldly. The multiplication of pleasures, the innumerable books that are being published, the newspaper pages filled with sporting events—surely, all these indicate that we constantly want to be amused. Because we are inwardly empty, dull, mediocre, we use our relationships and our social reforms as a means of escaping from ourselves. I wonder if you have noticed how lonely most people are? And to escape from loneliness we run to temples, churches, or mosques, we dress up and attend social functions, we watch television, listen to the radio, read, and so on.

Do you know what loneliness means? Some of you may be unfamiliar with that word, but you know the feeling very well. You try going out for a walk alone, or being without a book, without someone to talk to, and you will see how quickly you get bored. You know that feeling well enough, but you don't know *why* you get bored, you have never inquired into it. If you inquire a little into boredom you will find that the cause of it is loneliness. It is in order to escape from loneliness that we want to be together, we want to be entertained, to have distractions of every kind: *gurus*, religious ceremonies, prayers, or the latest novels. Being inwardly lonely we become mere spectators in life; and we can be the players only when we understand loneliness and go beyond it.

After all, most people marry and seek other social relationships because they don't know how to live alone. Not that one must live alone; but, if you marry because you want to be loved, or if you are bored and use your job as a means of forgetting yourself, then you will find that your whole life is nothing but an endless search for distractions. Very few go beyond this extraordinary fear of loneliness; but one *must* go beyond it, because beyond it lies the real treasure.

You know, there is a vast difference between loneliness and aloneness. Some of the younger students may still be unaware of loneliness, but the older people know it: the feeling of being utterly cut off, of suddenly being afraid without apparent cause. The mind knows this fear when for a moment it realizes that it can rely on nothing, that no distraction can take away the sense of self-enclosing emptiness. That is loneliness. But aloneness is something entirely different; it is a state of freedom which comes into being when you have gone through loneliness and understand it. In that state of aloneness you don't rely on anyone psychologically because you are no longer seeking pleasure, comfort, gratification. It is only then that the mind is completely alone, and only such a mind is creative.

All this is part of education: to face the ache of loneliness, that extraordinary feeling of emptiness which all of us know, and not be frightened when it comes; not to turn on the radio, lose oneself in work, or run to the cinema, but to look at it, go into it, understand it. There is no human being who has not felt or will not feel that quivering anxiety. It is because we try to run away from it through every form of distraction and gratification—through sex, through God, through work, through drink, through writing poems or repeating certain words which we have learnt by heart—that we never understand that anxiety when it comes upon us.

So, when the pain of loneliness comes upon you, confront it, look at it without any thought of running away. If you run away you will never understand it, and it will always be there waiting for you around the corner. Whereas, if you can understand loneliness and go beyond it, then you will find there is no need to escape, no urge to be gratified or entertained, for your mind will know a richness that is incorruptible and cannot be destroyed.

All this is part of education. If at school you merely learn subjects in order to pass examinations, then learning itself becomes a means of escape from loneliness. Think about it a little and you will see. Talk it over with your educators and you will soon find out how lonely they are, and how lonely you are. But those who are inwardly alone, whose minds and hearts are free from the ache of loneliness—they are real people, for they can discover for themselves what reality is, they can receive that which is timeless.

Questioner: What is the difference between awareness and sensitivity?

KRISHNAMURTI: I wonder if there is any difference? You know, when you ask a question, what is important is to find out for yourself the truth of the matter and not merely accept what someone else says. So let us find out together what it is to be aware.

You see a lovely tree with its leaves sparkling after the rain; you see the sunlight shining on the water and on the gray-hued feathers of the birds; you see the villagers walking to town carrying heavy burdens, and hear their laughter; you hear the bark of a dog, or a calf calling to its mother. All this is part of awareness, the awareness of what is around you, is it not? Coming a little closer, you notice your relationship to people, to ideas and to things;

you are aware of how you regard the house, the road; you observe your reactions to what people say to you, and how your mind is always evaluating, judging, comparing or condemning. This is all part of awareness, which begins on the surface and then goes deeper and deeper; but for most of us awareness stops at a certain point. We take in the noises, the songs, the beautiful and ugly sights, but we are not aware of our reactions to them. We say, "That is beautiful" or "That is ugly" and pass by; we don't inquire into what beauty is, what ugliness is. Surely, to see what your reactions are, to be more and more alert to every movement of your own thought, to observe that your mind is conditioned by the influence of your parents, of your teachers, of your race and culture—all this is part of awareness, is it not?

The deeper the mind penetrates its own thought processes, the more clearly it understands that all forms of thinking are conditioned; therefore the mind is spontaneously very still—which does not mean that it is asleep. On the contrary, the mind is then extraordinarily alert, no longer being drugged by *mantrams*, by the repetition of words, or shaped by discipline. This state of silent alertness is also part of awareness; and if you go into it still more deeply you will find that there is no division between the person who is aware and the object of which he is aware.

Now, what does it mean to be sensitive? To be cognizant of colour and form, of what people say and of your response to it; to be considerate, to have good taste, good manners; not to be rough, not to hurt people either physically or inwardly and be unaware of it; to see a beautiful thing and linger with it; to listen tentatively without being bored to everything that is said, so that the mind becomes acute, sharp—all this is sensitivity, is it not? So is there much difference between sensitivity and awareness? I don't think so.

You see, as long as your mind is condemning, judging, forming opinions, concluding, it is neither aware nor sensitive. When you are rude to people, when you pick flowers and throw them away, when you ill-treat animals, when you scratch your name on the furniture or break the leg of a chair, when you are unpunctual to meals and have bad manners in general, it all indicates insensitivity, does it not? It indicates a mind that is not capable of alert adjustment. And surely it is part of education to help the student to be sensitive, so that he will not merely conform or resist, but will be awake to the whole movement of life. The people who are sensitive in life may suffer much more than those who are insensitive; but if they understand and go beyond their suffering they will discover extraordinary things.

Questioner: Why do we laugh when somebody trips and falls?

KRISHNAMURTI: It is a form of insensitivity, is it not? Also there is such a thing as sadism. Do you know what that word means? An author called the Marquis de Sade once wrote a book about a man who enjoyed hurting people and seeing them suffer. From that comes the word 'sadism', which means deriving pleasure from the suffering of others. For certain people there is a peculiar satisfaction in seeing others suffer. Watch yourself and see if you have this feeling. It may not be obvious, but if it is there you will find that it expresses itself in the impulse to laugh when somebody falls. You want those who are high to be pulled down; you criticize, gossip thoughtlessly about others, all of which is an expression of insensitivity, a form of wanting to hurt people. One may injure another deliberately, with vengeance, or one may do it unconsciously with a word, with a gesture, with a look; but in either case the urge is to hurt somebody, and there are very few who radically set aside this perverted form of pleasure.

Questioner: One of our professors says that what you are telling us is quite impractical. He challenges you to bring up six boys and six girls on a salary of 120 rupees. What is your answer to this criticism?

KRISHNAMURTI: If I had only a salary of 120 rupees I would not attempt to raise six boys and six girls; that is the first thing. Secondly, if I were a professor it would be a dedication and not a job. Do you see the difference? Teaching at any level is not a profession, it is not a mere job; it is an act of dedication. Do you understand the meaning of that word "dedication"? To be dedicated is to give oneself to something completely, without asking anything in return; to be like a monk, like a hermit, like the great teachers and scientists—not like those who pass a few examinations and call themselves professors. I am talking of those who have dedicated themselves to teaching, not for money, but because it is their vocation, it is their love. If there are such teachers, they will find that boys and girls can be taught most practically all the things I am talking about. But the teacher, the educator, the professor to whom teaching is only a job for earning a living—it is he who will tell you that these things are not practical.

After all, what is practical? Think it out. The way we are living now, the way we are teaching, the way our governments are being run with their corruption and incessant wars—do you call *that* practical? Is ambition practical, is greed practical? Ambition breeds competition and therefore destroys people. A society based on greed and acquisition has always within it the spectre of war, conflict, suffering; and is *that* practical? Obviously it is not. That is what I am trying to tell you in all these various talks.

Love is the most practical thing in the world. To love, to be kind, not to be greedy, not to be ambitious, not to be influenced by people but to think for yourself—these are all very practical things, and they will bring about a practical, happy society. But the teacher who is not dedicated, who does not love, who may have a few letters after his name but is merely a purveyor of information which he has picked up from books—he will tell you that all this is not practical, because he has not really thought about it. To love is to be practical—far more so than the absurd practicality of this so-called education which produces citizens who are utterly incapable of standing alone and thinking out any problem for themselves.

You see, this is part of awareness: to be cognizant of the fact that they are giggling over there in the corner, and at the same time to continue with one's own seriousness.

The difficulty with most grown-up people is that they have not solved the problem of their own living, and yet they say to you, "I will tell you what is practical and what is not". Teaching is the greatest vocation in life, though now it is the most despised; it is the highest, the noblest of callings. But the teacher must be utterly dedicated, he must give himself to it completely, he must teach with his heart and mind, with his whole being; and out of that dedication things are made possible.

Questioner: What is the good of education if while being educated we are also being destroyed by the luxuries of the modern world?

KRISHNAMURTI: I am afraid you are using wrong words. One must have a certain amount of comfort, must one not? When one sits quietly in a room, it is well that the room be clean and tidy, though it may be utterly empty of all furniture but a mat; it should also be of good proportions and have windows of the right size. If there is a picture in the room it should be of something lovely, and if there is a flower in a vase it should have behind it the spirit of the person who placed it there. One also needs good food and a quiet place to sleep. All this is part of the comfort which is offered by the modern world; and is this comfort destroying the so-called educated man? Or is the so-called educated man, through his ambition and greed, destroying ordinary comfort for every human being? In the prosperous countries modern education is making people more and more materialistic, and therefore luxury in every form is perverting and destroying the mind; and in the poor countries, like India, education is not encouraging you to create a radically new kind of culture, it is not helping you to be a revolutionary. I have explained what I mean by a revolutionary—not the bomb-throwing, murderous kind. Such people are not revolutionaries. A true revolutionary is a man who is free of all inducement, free of ideologies and the entanglements of society which is an expression of the collective will of the many; and your education is not helping you to be a revolutionary of that kind. On the contrary, it is teaching you to conform, or merely to reform what is already there.

So it is your so-called education that is destroying you, not the luxury which the modern world provides. Why should you not have cars and good roads? But, you see, all the modern techniques and inventions are being used either for war, or merely for amusement, as a means of escape from oneself, and so the mind gets lost in gadgets. Modern education has become the cultivation of gadgets, the mechanical devices or machines which help you to cook, to clean, to iron, to calculate and do various other essential things, so that you don't have to think about them all the time. And you should have these gadgets, not to get lost in gadgetry, but to free your mind to do something totally different.

Questioner: I have a very black skin, and most people admire a lighter complexion. How can I win their admiration?

KRISHNAMURTI: I believe there are special cosmetics which are supposed to make your skin lighter; but will that solve your problem? You will still want to be admired, to be socially prominent, you will still long for position, prestige; and in the very demand for admiration, in the struggle for prominence, there is always the sting of sorrow. As long as you want to be admired, to be prominent, your education is going to destroy you, because it will help you to become somebody in this society, and this society is pretty rotten. We have built this destructive society through our greed, through our envy, through our fear, and it is not going to be transformed by ignoring it or calling it an illusion. Only the right kind of education will wipe away greed, fear, acquisitiveness, so that we can build a radically new culture, a different world altogether; and there can be the right kind of education only when the mind really wants to understand itself and be free of sorrow.

24

The Energy of Life

One of our most difficult problems is what we call discipline, and it is really very complex. You see, society feels that it must control or discipline the citizen, shape his mind according to certain religious, social, moral and economic patterns.

Now, is discipline necessary at all? Please listen carefully, don't immediately say "yes" or "no". Most of us feel, especially while we are young, that there should be no discipline, that we should be allowed to do whatever we like, and we think that is freedom. But merely to say that we should or should not have discipline, that we should be free, and so on, has very little meaning without understanding the whole problem of discipline.

The keen athlete is disciplining himself all the time, is he not? His joy in playing games and the very necessity to keep fit makes him go to bed early, refrain from smoking, eat the right food and generally observe the rules of good health. His discipline is not an imposition or a conflict, but a natural outcome of his enjoyment of athletics.

Now, does discipline increase or decrease human energy? Human beings throughout the world, in every religion, in every school of philosophy, impose discipline on the mind, which implies control, resistance, adjustment, suppression; and is all this necessary? If discipline brings about a greater output of human energy, then it is worth while, then it has meaning; but if it merely suppresses human energy, it is very harmful, destructive. All of us have energy, and the question is whether that energy through discipline can be made vital, rich and abundant, or whether discipline destroys whatever energy we have. I think this is the central issue.

Many human beings do not have a great deal of energy, and what little energy they have is soon smothered and destroyed by the controls, threats and taboos of their particular society with its so-called education; so they become imitative, lifeless citizens of that society. And does discipline give increased energy to the individual who has a little more to begin with? Does it make his life rich and full of vitality?

When you are very young, as you all are, you are full of energy, are you not? You want to play, to rush about, to talk; you can't sit still, you are full of life. Then what happens? As you grow up your teachers begin to curtail that energy by shaping it, directing it into various moulds; and when at last you become men and women the little energy you have left is soon smothered by society, which says that you must be proper citizens, you must behave in a certain way. Through so-called education and the compulsion of society this abounding energy you have when you are young is gradually destroyed.

Now, can the energy you have at present be made more vital through discipline? If you have only a little energy, can discipline increase it? If it can, then discipline has meaning; but if discipline really destroys one's energy, then discipline must obviously be put aside.

What is this energy which we all have? This energy is thinking, feeling; it is interest, enthusiasm, greed, passion, lust, ambition, hate. Painting pictures, inventing machines, building bridges, making roads, cultivating the fields, playing games, writing poems, singing, dancing, going to the temple, worshipping—these are all expressions of energy; and energy also creates illusion, mischief, misery. The very finest and the most destructive qualities are equally the expressions of human energy. But, you see, the process of controlling or disciplining this energy, letting it out in one direction and restricting it in another, becomes merely a social convenience; the mind is shaped according to the pattern of a particular culture, and thereby its energy is gradually dissipated.

So, our problem is, can this energy, which in one degree or another we all possess, be increased, given greater vitality—and if so, to do what? What is energy for? Is it the purpose of energy to make war? Is it to invent jet planes and innumerable other machines, to pursue some *guru*, to pass examinations, to have children, to worry endlessly over this problem and that? Or can energy be used in a different way so that all our activities have significance in relation to something which transcends them all? Surely, if the human mind, which is capable of such astonishing energy, is not seeking reality or God, then every expression of its energy becomes a means of destruction and misery. To seek reality requires immense energy; and, if man is not doing that, he dissipates his energy in ways which create mischief, and therefore society has to control him. Now, is it possible to liberate energy in seeking God or truth and, in the process of discovering what is true, to be a citizen who understands the fundamental issues of life and whom society cannot destroy? Are you following this, or is it a little bit too complex?

You see, man is energy, and if man does not seek truth, this energy becomes destructive; therefore society controls and shapes the individual, which smothers this energy. That is what has happened to the majority of grown-up people all over the world. And perhaps you have noticed another interesting and very simple fact: that the moment you really want to do something, you have the energy to do it. What happens when you are keen to play a game? You immediately have energy, have you not? And that very energy becomes the means of controlling itself, so you don't need outside discipline. In the search for reality, energy creates its own discipline. The man who is seeking reality spontaneously becomes the right kind of citizen, which is not according to the pattern of any particular society or government.

So, students as well as teachers must work together to bring about the release of this tremendous energy to find reality, God or truth. In your very seeking of truth there will be discipline, and then you will be a real human being, a complete individual, and not merely a Hindu or a Parsi limited by his particular society and culture. If, instead of curtailing his energy as it is doing now, the school can help the student to awaken his energy in the pursuit of truth, then you will find that discipline has quite a different meaning.

Why is it that in the home, in the classroom and in the hostel you are always being told what you must do and what you must not do? Surely, it is because your parents and teachers, like the rest of society, have not perceived that man exists for only one purpose, which is to find reality or God. If even a small group of educators were to understand and give their whole attention to that search, they would create a new kind of education and a different society altogether.

Don't you notice how little energy most of the people around you have, including your parents and teachers? They are slowly dying, even when their bodies are not yet old. Why? Because they have been beaten into submission by society. You see, without understanding its fundamental purpose which is to free the extraordinary thing called the mind, with its capacity to create atomic submarines and jet planes, which can write the most amazing poetry and prose, which can make the world so beautiful and also destroy the world—without understanding the fundamental purpose, which is to find truth or God, this energy becomes destructive; and then society says, "We must shape and control the energy of the individual."

So, it seems to me that the function of education is to bring about a release of energy in the pursuit of goodness, truth, or God, which in turn makes the individual a true human being and therefore the right kind of citizen. But mere discipline, without full comprehension of all this, has no meaning, it is a most destructive thing. Unless each one of you is so educated that, when you leave school and go out into the world, you are full of vitality and intelligence, full of abounding energy to find out what is true, you will merely be absorbed by society; you will be smothered, destroyed, miserably unhappy for the rest of your life. As a river creates the banks which hold it, so the energy which seeks truth creates its own discipline without any form of imposition; and as the river finds the sea, so that energy finds its own freedom.

Questioner: Why did the British come to rule India?

KRISHNAMURTI: You see, the people who have more energy, more vitality, more capacity, more spirit, bring either misery or well-being to their less energetic neighbours. At one time India exploded all over Asia; her people were full of creative zeal, and they brought religion to China, to Japan, to Indonesia, to Burma. Other nations were commercial, which may have also been necessary, and which had its miseries—but that is the way of life. The strange part of it is that those who are seeking truth or God are much more explosive, they release extraordinary energy, not only in themselves but in others; and it is they who are the real revolutionaries, not the communists, the socialists, or those who merely reform. Conquerors and rulers come and go, but the human problem is ever the same. We all want to dominate, to submit or resist; but the man who is seeking truth is free of all societies and of all cultures.

Questioner: Even at the time of meditation one doesn't seem able to perceive what is true; so will you please tell us what is true?

KRISHNAMURTI: Let us leave for the moment the question of what is true and consider first what is meditation. To me, meditation is something entirely different from what your books and your *gurus* have taught you. Meditation is the process of understanding your own mind. If you don't understand your own thinking, which is self-knowledge, whatever you think has very little meaning. Without the foundation of self-knowledge, thinking leads to mischief. Every thought has a significance; and if the mind is incapable of seeing the significance, not just of one or two thoughts, but of each thought as it arises then merely to concentrate on a particular idea, image, or set of words—which is generally called meditation—is a form of self-hypnosis.

So, whether you are sitting quietly, talking, or playing, are you aware of the significance of every thought, of every reaction that you happen to have? Try it and you will see how difficult it is to be aware of every movement of your own thought, because thoughts pile up so quickly one on top of another. But if you want to examine every thought, if you really want to see the content of it, then you will find that your thoughts slow down and you can watch them. This slowing down of thinking and the examining of every thought is the process of meditation; and if you go into it you will find that, by being aware of every thought, your mind—which is now a vast storehouse of restless thoughts all battling against each other—becomes very quiet, completely still. There is then no urge, no compulsion, no fear in any form; and, in this stillness, that which is true comes into being. There is no "you" who experiences truth, but the mind being still, truth comes into it. The moment there is a "you" there is the experiencer, and the experiencer is merely the result of thought, he has no basis without thinking.

Questioner: If we make a mistake and somebody points it out to us, why do we commit the same error again?

KRISHNAMURTI: What do *you* think? Why do you pick at the flowers, or tear up plants, or destroy furniture, or throw paper about, though I am sure you have been told a dozen times that you should not do it? Listen carefully and you will see. When you do such things you are in a state of thoughtlessness, are you not? You are not aware, you are not thinking, your mind has gone to sleep, and so you do things which are obviously stupid. As long as you are not fully conscious, not completely *there*, it is no good merely telling you not to do certain things. But, if the educator can help you to be thoughtful, to be really aware, to observe with delight the trees, the birds, the river, the extraordinary richness of the earth, then one hint will be enough, because then you will be sensitive, alive to everything about you and within yourself.

Unfortunately, your sensitivity is destroyed because, from the time you are born till you die, you are everlastingly being told to do this and not to do that. Parents, teachers, society, religion, the priest, and also your own ambitions, your own greeds and envies—they all say "do" and "don't". To be free of all these *do's* and *don'ts* and yet to be sensitive so that you are spontaneously kind and do not hurt people, do not throw paper about or pass by a rock on the road without removing it—this requires great thoughtfulness. And the purpose of education, surely, is not just to give you a few letters of the alphabet after your name, but to awaken in you this spirit of thoughtfulness so that you are sensitive, alert, watchful, kind.

Questioner: What is life, and how can we be happy?

KRISHNAMURTI: A very good question from a little boy. What is life? If you ask the business man, he will tell you that life is a matter of selling things, making money, because that is his life from morning till night. The man of ambition will tell you that life is a struggle to achieve, to fulfil. For the man who has attained position and power, who is the head of an organization or a country, life is full of activity of his own making. And for the labourer, especially in this country, life is endless work without a day of rest; it is to be dirty, miserable, without sufficient food.

Now, can man be happy through all this strife, this struggle, this starvation and misery? Obviously not. So what does he do? He does not question, he does not ask what life is, but philosophizes about happiness. He talks about brotherhood while exploiting others. He invents the higher self, the super-soul, something which eventually is going to make him permanently happy. But happiness does not come into being when you seek it; it is a by-product, it comes into being when there is goodness, when there is love, when there is no ambition, when the mind is quietly seeking out what is true.

Questioner: Why do we fight among ourselves?

KRISHNAMURTI: I think the older people also ask this question, don't they? Why do we fight? America is opposed to Russia, China stands against the West. Why? We talk about peace and prepare for war. Why? Because I think the majority of human beings love to compete, to fight, that is the plain fact, otherwise we would stop it. In fighting there is a heightened sense of being alive, that also is a fact. We think struggle in every form is necessary to keep us alive; but, you see, that kind of living is very destructive. There is a way of living without struggle. It is like the lily, like the flower that grows; it does not struggle, it *is*. The being of anything is the goodness of it. But we are not educated for that at all. We are educated to compete, to fight, to be soldiers, lawyers, policemen, professors, principals, business men, all wanting to ride on top. We all want success. There are many who have the outward pretensions of humility, but only those are happy who are really humble inwardly, and it is they who do not fight.

Questioner: Why does the mind misuse other human beings and also misuse itself?

KRISHNAMURTI: What do we mean by misuse? A mind that is ambitious, greedy, envious, a mind that is burdened with belief and tradition, a mind that is ruthless, that exploits people—such a mind in its action obviously creates mischief and brings about a society which is full of conflict. As long as the mind does not understand itself, its action is bound to be destructive; as long as the mind has no self-knowledge, it must breed enmity. That is why it is essential that you should come to know yourself and not merely learn from books. No book can teach you self-knowledge. A book may give you information about self-knowledge, but that is not the same thing as knowing yourself in action. When the mind sees itself in the mirror of relationship, from that perception there is self-knowledge; and without self-knowledge we cannot clear up this mess, this terrible misery which we have created in the world.

Questioner: Is the mind that seeks success different from that which seeks truth?

KRISHNAMURTI: It is the same mind, whether it is seeking success or truth; but, as long as the mind is seeking success, it cannot find out what is true. To understand the truth is to see the truth in the false, and to see what is true as true.

25

To Live Effortlessly

Have you ever wondered why it is that as people grow older they seem to lose all joy in life? At present most of you who are young are fairly happy; you have your little problems, there are examinations to worry about, but in spite of these troubles there is in your life a certain joy, is there not? There is a spontaneous, easy acceptance of life, a looking at things lightly and happily. And why is it that as we grow older we seem to lose that joyous intimation of something beyond, something of greater significance? Why do so many of us, as we grow into so-called maturity became dull, insensitive to joy, to beauty, to the open skies and the marvellous earth?

You know, when one asks oneself this question, many explanations spring up in the mind. We are so concerned with ourselves—that is one explanation. We struggle to become somebody, to achieve and maintain a certain position; we have children and other responsibilities, and we have to earn money. All these external things soon weigh us down, and thereby we lose the joy of living. Look at the older faces around you, see how sad most of them are, how careworn and rather ill, how withdrawn, aloof and sometimes neurotic, without a smile. Don't you ask yourself why? And even when we do ask why, most of us seem to be satisfied with mere explanations.

Yesterday evening I saw a boat going up the river at full sail, driven by the west wind. It was a large boat, heavily laden with firewood for the town. The sun was setting, and this boat against the sky was astonishingly beautiful. The boatman was just guiding it, there was no effort, for the wind was doing all the work. Similarly, if each one of us could understand the problem of struggle and conflict, then I think we would be able to live effortlessly, happily, with a smile on our face.

I think it is effort that destroys us, this struggling in which we spend almost every moment of our lives. If you watch the older people around you, you will see that for most of them life is a series of battles with themselves, with their wives or husbands, with their neighbours, with society; and this ceaseless strife dissipates energy. The man who is joyous, really happy, is not caught up in effort. To be without effort does not mean that you stagnate, that you are dull, stupid; on the contrary, it is only the wise, the extraordinarily intelligent who are really free of effort, of struggle.

But, you see, when we hear of effortlessness we want to be like that, we want to achieve a state in which we will have no strife, no conflict; so we make that our goal, our ideal, and strive after it; and the moment we do this, we have lost the joy of living. We are again caught up in effort, struggle. The object of struggle varies, but all struggle is essentially the same. One may struggle to bring about social reforms, or to find God, or to create a better relationship between oneself, and one's wife or husband, or with one's neighbour; one may sit on the bank of Ganga, worship at the feet of some *guru*, and so on. All this is effort, struggle. So what is important is not the object of struggle, but to understand struggle, itself.

Now, is it possible for the mind to be not just casually aware that for the moment it is not struggling, but completely free of struggle all the time so that it discovers a state of joy in which there is no sense of the superior and the inferior?

Our difficulty is that the mind feels inferior, and that is why it struggles to be or become something, or to bridge over its various contradictory desires. But don't let us give explanations of why the mind is full of struggle. Every thinking man knows why there is struggle both within and without. Our envy, greed, ambition, our competitiveness leading to ruthless efficiency—these are obviously the factors which cause us to struggle, whether in this world or in the world to come. So we don't have to study psychological books to know why we struggle; and what is important, surely, is to find out if the mind can be totally free of struggle.

After all, when we struggle, the conflict is between what we are and what we *should* be or *want* to be. Now, without giving explanations, can one understand this whole process of struggle so that it comes to an end? Like that boat which was moving with the wind, can the mind be without struggle? Surely, this is the question, and not how to achieve a state in which there is no struggle. The very effort to achieve such a state is itself a process of struggle, therefore that state is never achieved. But if you observe from moment to moment how the mind gets caught in everlasting struggle—if you just observe the fact without trying to alter it, without trying to force upon the mind a certain state which you call peace—then you will find that the mind spontaneously ceases to struggle; and in that state it can learn enormously. Learning is then not merely the process of gathering information, but a discovery of the extraordinary riches that lie beyond the scope of the mind; and for the mind that makes this discovery there is joy.

Watch yourself and you will see how you struggle from morning till night, and how your energy is wasted in this struggle. If you merely explain why you struggle, you get lost in explanations and the struggle continues; whereas, if you observe your mind very quietly without giving explanations, if you just let the mind be aware of its own struggle, you will soon find that there comes a state in which there is no struggle at all, but an astonishing watchfulness. In that state of watchfulness there is no sense of the superior and the inferior, there is no big man or little man, there is no *guru.* All those absurdities are gone because the mind is fully awake; and the mind that is fully awake is joyous.

Questioner: I want to do a certain thing, and though I have tried many times I have not been successful in doing it. Should I give up striving, or should I persist in this effort?

KRISHNAMURTI: To be successful is to arrive, to get somewhere; and we worship success, do we not? When a poor boy grows up and becomes a multi-millionaire, or an ordinary student becomes the prime minister, he is applauded, made much of; so every boy and girl wants in one way or another to succeed.

Now, is there such a thing as success, or is it only an idea which man pursues? Because the moment you arrive there is always a point further ahead at which you have yet to arrive. As long as you pursue success in any direction you are bound to be in strife, in conflict, are you not? Even when you have arrived, there is no rest for you, because you want to go still higher, you want to have more. Do you understand? The pursuit of success is the desire for the "more", and a mind that is constantly demanding the "more" is not an intelligent mind; on the contrary, it is a mediocre, stupid mind, because its demand for the "more" implies a constant struggle in terms of the pattern which society has set for it.

After all, what is contentment, and what is discontent? Discontent is the striving after the "more", and contentment is the cessation of that struggle; but you cannot come to contentment without understanding the whole process of the "more", and why the mind demands it.

If you fail in an examination, for example, you have to take it again, do you not? Examinations in any case are most unfortunate, because they don't indicate anything significant, they don't reveal the true worth of your intelligence. Passing an examination is largely a trick of memory, or it may be a matter of chance; but you strive to pass your examinations, and if you don't succeed you keep at it. With most of us it is the same process in everyday life. We are struggling after something, and we have never paused to inquire if the thing we are after is worth struggling for. We have never asked ourselves if it's worth the effort, so we haven't yet discovered that it's not and withstood the opinion of our parents, of society, of all the Masters and *gurus*. It is only when we have understood the whole significance of the 'more' that we cease to think in terms of failure and success.

You see, we are so afraid to fail, to make mistakes, not only in examinations but in life. To make a mistake is considered terrible because we will be criticized for it, somebody will scold us. But, after all, why should you not make a mistake? Are not all the people in the world making mistakes? And would the world cease to be in this horrible mess if you were never to make a mistake? If you are afraid of making mistakes you will never learn. The older people are making mistakes all the time, but they don't want *you* to make mistakes, and thereby they smother your initiative. Why? Because they are afraid that by observing and questioning everything, by experimenting and making mistakes you may find out something for yourself and break away from the authority of your parents, of society, of tradition. That is why the ideal of success is held up for you to follow; and success, you will notice, is always in terms of respectability. Even the saint in his so-called spiritual achievements must become respectable, otherwise he has no recognition, no following.

So we are always thinking in terms of success, in terms of the "more"; and the "more" is evaluated by the respectable society. In other words, society has very carefully established a certain pattern according to which it pronounces you a success or a failure. But if you love to do something with all your being you are then not concerned with success and failure. No intelligent person is. But unfortunately there are very few intelligent people, and nobody tells you about all this. The whole concern of an intelligent person is to see the facts and understand the problem—which is not to think in terms of succeeding or failing. It is only when we don't really love what we are doing that we think in those terms.

Questioner: Why are we fundamentally selfish? We may try our best to be unselfish in our behaviour, but when our own interests are involved we become self-absorbed and indifferent to the interests of others.

KRISHNAMURTI: I think it is very important not to call oneself either selfish or unselfish, because words have an extraordinary influence on the mind. Call a man selfish, and he is doomed; call him a professor, and something happens in your approach to him; call him a Mahatma, and immediately there is a halo around him. Watch your own responses and you will see that words like "lawyer", "business man", "governor", "servant", "love", "God", have a strange effect on your nerves as well as on your mind. The word which denotes a particular function evokes the feeling of status; so the first thing is to be free of this unconscious habit of associating certain feelings with certain words, is it not? Your mind has been conditioned to think that the term "selfish" represents something very wrong, unspiritual, and the moment you apply that term to anything your mind condemns it. So when you ask this question, "Why are we fundamentally selfish?", it has already a condemnatory significance.

It is very important to be aware that certain words cause in you a nervous, emotional, or intellectual response of approval or condemnation. When you call yourself a jealous person, for example, immediately you have blocked further inquiry, you have stopped penetrating into the whole problem of jealousy. Similarly, there are many people who say they are working for brotherhood, yet everything they do is against brotherhood; but they don't see this fact because the word 'brotherhood' means something to them and they are already persuaded by it; they don't inquire any further and so they never find out what are the facts irrespective of the neurological or emotional response which that word evokes.

So this is the first thing: to experiment and find out if you can look at facts without the condemnatory or laudatory implications associated with certain words. If you can look at the facts without feelings of condemnation or approval, you will find that in the very process of looking there is a dissolution of all the barriers which the mind has erected between itself and the facts.

Just observe how you approach a person whom people call a great man. The words "great man" have influenced you; the newspapers, the books, the followers all say he is a great man, and your mind has accepted it. Or else you take the opposite view and say, "How stupid, he is *not* a great man". Whereas, if you can dissociate your mind from all influence and simply look at the facts, then you will find that your approach is entirely different. In the same way, the word "villager", with its associations of poverty, dirt, squalor, or whatever it is, influences your thinking. But when the mind is free of influence, when it neither condemns nor approves but merely looks, observes, then it is not self-absorbed and there is no longer the problem of selfishness trying to be unselfish.

Questioner: Why is it that, from birth to death, the individual always wants to be loved, and that if he doesn't get this love he is not as composed and full of confidence as his fellow beings?

KRISHNAMURTI: Do you think that his fellow beings are full of confidence? They may strut about, they may put on airs, but you will find that behind the show of confidence most people are empty, dull, mediocre, they have no real confidence at all. And why do we want to be loved? Don't you want to be loved by your parents, by your teachers, by your friends? And, if you are a grown-up, you want to be loved by your wife, by your husband, by your children—or by your *guru*. Why is there this everlasting craving to be loved? Listen carefully. You want to be loved because you do not love; but the moment you love, it is finished, you are no longer inquiring whether or not somebody loves you. As long as you demand to be loved, there is no love in you; and if you feel no love, you are ugly, brutish, so why should you be loved? Without love you are a dead thing; and when the dead thing asks for love, it is still dead. Whereas, if your heart is full of love, then you never ask to be loved, you never put out your begging bowl for someone to fill it. It is only the empty who ask to be filled, and an empty heart can never be filled by running after *gurus* or seeking love in a hundred other ways.

Questioner: Why do grown-up people steal?

KRISHNAMURTI: Don't you sometimes steal? Haven't you known of a little boy stealing something he wants from another boy? It is exactly the same throughout life, whether we are young or old, only the older people do it more cunningly, with a lot of fine-sounding words; they want wealth, power, position, and they connive, contrive, philosophize to get it. They steal, but it is not called stealing, it is called by some respectable word. And why do we steal? First of all, because, as society is now constituted, it deprives many people of the necessities of life; certain sections of the populace have insufficient food, clothing and shelter, therefore they do something about it. There are also those who steal, not because they have insufficient food, but because they are what is called anti-social. For them stealing has become a game, a form of excitement—which means that they have had no real education. Real education is understanding the significance of life, not just cramming to pass examinations. There is also stealing at a higher level: the stealing of other people's ideas, the stealing of knowledge. When we are after the "more" in any form, we are obviously stealing.

Why is it that we are always asking, begging, wanting, stealing? Because in ourselves there is nothing; inwardly, psychologically we are like an empty drum. Being empty, we try to fill ourselves, not only by stealing things, but by imitating others. Imitation is a form of stealing: you are nothing but he is somebody, so you are going to get some of his glory by copying him. This corruption runs right through human life, and very few are free of it. So what is important is to find out whether the inward emptiness can ever be filled. As long as the mind is seeking to fill itself, it will always be empty. When the mind is no longer concerned with filling its own emptiness, then only does that emptiness cease to be.

26

The Mind Is Not Everything

You know, it is so nice just to be very quiet, to sit up straight with dignity, with poise—and that is as important as it is to look at those leafless trees. Have you noticed how lovely those trees are against the pale blue of the morning sky? The naked branches of a tree reveal its beauty; and trees also have an extraordinary beauty about them in the spring, in the summer and in the autumn. Their beauty changes with the seasons, and to notice this is as important as it is to consider the ways of our own life.

Whether we live in Russia, in America, or in India, we are all human beings; as human beings we have common problems, and it is absurd to think of ourselves as Hindus, Americans, Russians, Chinese, and so on. There are political, geographic, racial and economic divisions, but to emphasize the divisions only breeds antagonism and hatred. Americans may be for the moment far more prosperous, which means that they have more gadgets, more radios, more television sets, more of everything including a surplus of food, while in this country there is so much starvation, squalor, over-population and unemployment. But wherever we live we are all human beings, and as human beings we create our own human problems; and it is very important to understand that in thinking of ourselves as Hindus, Americans, or Englishmen, or as white, brown, black or yellow, we are creating needless barriers between ourselves.

One of our main difficulties is that modern education all over the world is chiefly concerned with making us mere technicians. We learn how to design jet planes, how to construct paved roads, how to build cars or run the latest nuclear submarines, and in the midst of all this technology we forget that we are human beings—which means that we are filling our hearts with the things of the mind. In America automation is releasing more and more people from long hours of labour, as it will presently be doing in this country, and then we shall have the immense problem of how to utilize our time. Huge factories now employing many thousands will probably be run by a few technicians; and what is to become of all the other human beings who used to work there and who will have so much time on their hands? Until education begins to take this and other human problems into account, our lives will be very empty.

Our lives are very empty now, are they not? You may have a college degree, you may get married and be well off, you may be very clever, have a great deal of information, know the latest books; but as long as you fill your heart with the things of the mind, your life is bound to be empty, ugly, and it will have very little meaning. There is beauty and meaning in life only when the heart is cleansed of the things of the mind.

You see, all this is our own individual problem, it is not some speculative problem that doesn't concern us. If as human beings we don't know how to care for the earth and the things of the earth, if we don't know how to love our children and are merely concerned with ourselves, with our personal or national advancement and success, we shall make our world hideous—which is what we are already doing. One country may become very rich, but its riches are a poison as long as there is another country which is starving. We are one humanity, the earth is ours to share, and with loving care it will produce food, clothing and shelter for us all.

So, the function of education is not merely to prepare you to pass a few examinations, but to help you understand this whole problem of living—in which is included sex, earning a livelihood, laughter, having initiative, being earnest and knowing how to think deeply. It is also our problem to find out what God is, because that is the very foundation of our life. A house cannot stand for long without a proper foundation, and all the cunning inventions of man will be meaningless if we are not seeking out what is God or truth.

The educator must be capable of helping you to understand this, for you have to begin in childhood, not when you are sixty. You will never find God at sixty, for at that age most people are worn out, finished. You must begin when you are very young, because then you can lay the right foundation so that your house will stand through all the storms that human beings create for themselves. Then you can live happily because your happiness is not dependent on anything, it is not dependent on *saris* and jewels, on cars and radios, on whether somebody loves or rejects you. You are happy not because you possess something, not because you have position, wealth, or learning, but because your life has meaning in itself. But that meaning is discovered only when you are seeking out reality from moment to moment—and reality is in everything, it is not to be found in the church, in the temple, in the mosque, or in some ritual.

To seek out reality we must know how to go about removing the dust of centuries that has settled upon it; and please believe me, that search for reality is true education. Any clever man can read books and accumulate information, achieve a position and exploit others, but that is not education. The study of certain subjects is merely a very small part of education; but there is a vast area of our life for which we are not educated at all, and to which we have no right approach.

To find out how to approach life so that our daily living, our radios, cars and airplanes have a meaning in relationship to something else which includes and transcends them all—*that* is education. In other words, education must begin with religion. But religion has nothing to do with the priest, with the church, with any dogma or belief. Religion is to love without motive, to be generous, to be good, for only then are we real human beings; but goodness, generosity, or love does not come into being save through the search for reality.

Unfortunately, this whole vast field of life is ignored by the so-called education of today. You are constantly occupied with books which have very little meaning, and with passing examinations which have still less meaning. They may get you a job, and that does have some meaning. But presently many factories will be run almost entirely by machines, and that is why we must begin now to be educated to use our leisure rightly—not in the pursuit of ideals, but to discover and understand the vast areas of our existence of which we are now unconscious and know nothing. The mind, with its cunning arguments, is not everything. There is something vast and immeasurable beyond the mind, a loveliness which the mind cannot understand. In that immensity there is an ecstasy, a glory; and the living in that, the experiencing of that is the way of education. Unless you have that kind of education, when you go out into the world you will perpetuate this hideous mess which past generations have created.

So, teachers and students, do think about all this. Don't complain, but put your shoulder to the wheel and help to create an institution where religion, in the right sense, is investigated, loved, worked out and lived. Then you will find that life becomes astonishingly rich—far richer than all the bank accounts in the world.

Questioner: How did man come to have so much knowledge? How did he evolve materially? Whence does he draw such vast energies?

KRISHNAMURTI: "How did man come to have so much knowledge?" That is fairly simple. You know something and pass it on to your children; they add a little more and pass it on to *their* children, and so on down through the ages. We gather knowledge little by little. Our great grandfathers did not know a thing about jet planes and the electronic marvels of today; but curiosity, necessity, war, fear and greed have brought about all this knowledge by degrees.

Now, there is a peculiar thing about knowledge. You may know a great deal, gather vast stores of information; but a mind that is clouded by knowledge, burdened with information, is incapable of discovery. It may use a discovery through knowledge and technique, but the discovery itself is something original which suddenly bursts upon the mind irrespective of knowledge; and it is this explosion of discovery that is essential. Most people, especially in this country, are so smothered by knowledge, by tradition, by opinion, by fear of what their parents or neighbours will say, that they have no confidence. They are like dead people—and that is what the burden of knowledge does to the mind. Knowledge is useful, but without something else it is also most destructive, and this is being shown by world events at the present time.

Look at what is happening in the world. There are all these marvellous inventions: radar which detects the approach of an airplane while still many miles away;

submarines which can go submerged right around the world without once coming up; the miracle of being able to talk from Bombay to Banaras or New York, and so on. All this is the outcome of knowledge. But something else is missing, and therefore knowledge is misused; there is war, destruction, misery, and countless millions of people go hungry. They have only one meal a day, or even less—and you know nothing about all this. You only know your books and your own petty problems and pleasures in a particular corner of Banaras, Delhi, or Bombay. You see, we may have a great deal of knowledge, but without that something else by which man lives and in which there is joy, glory, ecstasy, we are going to destroy ourselves.

Materially it is the same thing: man has evolved materially through a gradual process. And whence does he draw such vast energies? The great inventors, the explorers and discoverers in every field must have had enormous energy; but most of us have very little energy, have we not? While we are young we play games, we have fun, we dance and sing; but when we grow up that energy is soon destroyed. Have you not noticed it? We become weary housewives, or we go to an office for endless hours day after day, month in and month out, merely to earn a livelihood; so naturally we have little or no energy. If we had energy we might destroy this rotten society, we might do the most disturbing things; therefore society sees to it that we don't have energy, it gradually smothers us through "education", through tradition, through so-called religion and culture. You see, the function of real education is to awaken our energy and make it explode, make it continuous, strong, passionate, and yet have spontaneous restraint and employ itself in the discovery of reality. Then that energy becomes immense, boundless, and it does not cause further misery but is in itself creator of a new society.

Do listen to what I am saying, don't brush it aside, because it is really important. Don't just agree or disagree, but find out for yourself if there is truth in what is being said. Don't be indifferent: be either hot or cold. If you see the truth of all this and are really hot about it, that heat, that energy will grow and bring about a new society. It will not dissipate itself by merely revolting within the present society, which is like decorating the walls of a prison.

So our problem, especially in education, is how to maintain whatever energy we have and give it more vitality, a greater exploding force. This is going to require a great deal of understanding, because the teachers themselves generally have very little energy; they are smothered with mere information and are all but drowned in their own problems, therefore they cannot help the student to awaken this creative energy. That is why the understanding of these things is as much the teacher's concern as it is the student's.

Questioner: Why do my parents get angry when I say that I want to follow another religion?

KRISHNAMURTI: First of all, they are attached to their own religion, they think it is the best if not the only religion in the world, so naturally they want you also to follow it. Furthermore, they want you to adhere to their particular manner of thinking, to their group, their race, their class. These are some of the reasons; and also, you see, if you followed another religion you would become a nuisance, a trouble to the family.

But what has happened even when you do leave one organized religion to follow another? Have you not merely moved to another prison? You see, as long as the mind clings to a belief, it is held in a prison. If you are born a Hindu and become a Christian your parents may get angry, but that is a minor point. What is important is to see that when you join another religion you have merely taken on a new set of dogmas in place of the old. You may be a little more active, a little more this or that, but you are still within the prison of belief and dogma.

So don't exchange religions, which is merely to revolt within the prison, but break through the prison walls and find out for yourself what is God, what is truth. *That* has meaning, and it will give you enormous vitality, energy. But merely to go from one prison to another and quarrel about which prison is better—this is a child's game.

To break out of the prison of belief requires a mature mind, a thoughtful mind, a mind that perceives the nature of the prison itself and does not compare one prison with another. To understand something you cannot compare it with something else. Understanding does not come through comparison, it comes only when you examine the thing itself. If you examine the nature of organized religion you will see that all religions are essentially alike, whether Hinduism, Buddhism, Mohammedanism, Christianity—or communism, which is another form of religion, the very latest. The moment you understand the prison, which is to perceive all the implications of belief, of rituals and priests, you will never again belong to any religion; because only the man who is free of belief can discover that which lies beyond all belief, that which is immeasurable.

Questioner: What is the real way to build up character?

KRISHNAMURTI: To have character means, surely, to be able to withstand the false and hold on to the true; but to build character is difficult, because for most of us what is said by the book, by the teacher, by the parent, by the government is more important than to find out what we ourselves think. To think for oneself, to find out what is true and stand by it, without being influenced, whatever life may bring of misery or happiness—that is what builds character.

Say, for instance, you do not believe in war, not because of what some reformer or religious teacher has said, but because you have thought it out for yourself. You have investigated, gone into the question, meditated upon it, and for you all killing is wrong, whether it is killing to eat, killing out of hatred, or killing for the so-called love of one's country. Now, if you feel this very strongly and stick to it in spite of everything, regardless of whether you go to prison or are shot for it, as you may be in certain countries, then you will have character. Then character has quite a different meaning, it is not the character which society cultivates.

But, you see, we are not encouraged in this direction; and neither the educator nor the student has the vitality, the energy to think out and see what is true, and hold to it, letting the false go. But if you can do this then you won't follow any political or religious leader, because you will be a light unto yourself; and the discovery and cultivation of that light, not only while you are young but throughout life, is education.

Questioner: How does age stand in the way of realizing God?

KRISHNAMURTI: What is age? Is it the number of years you have lived? That is part of age; you were born in such and such a year, and now you are fifteen, forty or sixty years old. Your body grows old—and so does your mind when it is burdened with all the experiences, miseries and weariness of life; and such a mind can never discover what is truth. The mind can discover only when it is young, fresh, innocent; but innocence is not a matter of age. It is not only the child that is innocent—he may not be—but the mind that is capable of experiencing without accumulating the residue of experience. The mind must experience, that is inevitable. It must respond to everything—to the river, to the diseased animal, to the dead body being carried away to be burnt, to the poor villagers carrying their burdens along the road, to the tortures and miseries of life—otherwise it is already dead; but it must be capable of responding without being held by the experience. It is tradition, the accumulation of experience, the ashes of memory, that make the mind old. The mind that dies every day to the memories of yesterday, to all the joys and sorrows of the past—such a mind is fresh, innocent, it has no age; and without that innocence, whether you are ten or sixty, you will not find God.

27
To Seek God

One of the many problems confronting all of us, and especially those who are now being educated and must soon go out and face the world, is this question of reform. Various groups of people—the socialists, the communists, and reformers of every kind—are concerned with trying to bring about certain changes in the world, changes which are obviously necessary. Although in some countries there is a fair degree of prosperity, throughout the world there is still hunger, starvation, and millions of human beings have insufficient clothing and no proper place to sleep. And how is a fundamental reformation to take place without creating more chaos, more misery and strife? That is the real problem, is it not? If one reads a little history and observes present-day political trends, it becomes obvious that what we call reformation, however desirable and necessary, always brings in its wake still other forms of confusion and conflict; and to counteract this further misery, more legislation, more checks and counterchecks become necessary. Reformation creates new disorders; in putting these right, still further disorders are produced, and so the vicious circle continues. This is what we are faced with, and it is a process which seems to have no end.

Now, how is one to break through this vicious circle? Mind you, it is obvious that reformation is necessary;

but is reformation possible without bringing about still further confusion? This seems to me to be one of the fundamental issues with which any thoughtful person must be concerned. The question is not what kind of reformation is necessary, or at what level, but whether any reformation is possible at all without bringing with it other problems which again create the need of reform. And what is one to do in order to break up this endless process? Surely, it is the function of education, whether in the small school or in the large university, to tackle this problem, not abstractly, theoretically, not by merely philosophizing or writing books about it, but by actually facing it in order to find out how to solve it. Man is caught in this vicious circle of reformation which always needs further reform and, if it is not broken up, our problems can have no solution.

So, what kind of education, what kind of thinking is necessary to break up this vicious circle? What action will put an end to the increase of problems in all our activities? Is there any movement of thought, in any direction, that can free man from this manner of living, the reformation of which always needs further reform? In other words, is there an action which is not born of reaction?

I think there is a way of life in which there is not this process of reformation breeding further misery, and that way may be called religious. The truly religious person is not concerned with reform, he is not concerned with merely producing a change in the social order; on the contrary, he is seeking what is true, and that very search has a transforming effect on society. That is why education must be principally concerned with helping the student to seek out truth or God, and not merely preparing him to fit into the pattern of a given society.

I think it is very important to understand this while we are young; because, as we grow older and begin to set aside our little amusements and distractions, our sexual appetites and petty ambitions, we become more keenly aware of the immense problems confronting the world, and then we want to do something about them, we want to bring about some kind of amelioration. But unless we are deeply religious we shall only create more confusion, further misery; and religion has nothing to do with priests, churches, dogmas, or organized beliefs. These things are not religion at all, they are merely social conveniences to hold us within a particular pattern of thought and action; they are the means of exploiting our credulity, hope and fear. Religion is the seeking out of what is truth, what is God, and this search requires enormous energy, wide intelligence, subtle thinking. It is in this very seeking of the immeasurable that there is right social action, not in the so-called reformation of a particular society.

To find out what is truth there must be great love and a deep awareness of man's relationship to all things—which means that one is not concerned with one's own progress and achievements. The search for truth is true religion, and the man who is seeking truth is the only religious man. Such a man, because of his love, is outside of society, and his action upon society is therefore entirely different from that of the man who is in society and concerned with its reformation. The reformer can never create a new culture. What is necessary is the search of the truly religious man, for this very search brings about its own culture and it is our only hope. You see, the search for truth gives an explosive creativeness to the mind, which is true revolution, because in this search the mind is uncontaminated by the edicts and sanctions of society. Being free of all that, the religious man is able to find out what is true; and it is the discovery of what is true from moment to moment that creates a new culture.

That is why it is very important for you to have the right kind of education. For this the educator himself must be rightly educated so that he will not regard teaching merely as a means of earning a livelihood, but will be capable of helping the student to put aside all dogmas and not be held by any religion or belief. The people who come together on the basis of religious authority, or to practise certain ideals, are all concerned with social reform, which is merely the decorating of the prison walls. Only the truly religious man is truly revolutionary; and it is the function of education to help each one of us to be religious in the true sense of the word, for in that direction alone lies our salvation.

Questioner: I want to do social work, but I don't know how to start.

KRISHNAMURTI: I think it is very important to find out not how to start, but why you want to do social work at all. Why do you want to do social work? Is it because you see misery in the world—starvation, disease, exploitation, the brutal indifference of great wealth side by side with appalling poverty, the enmity between man and man? Is that the reason? Do you want to do social work because in your heart there is love and therefore you are not concerned with your own fulfilment? Or is social work a means of escape from yourself? Do you understand? You see, for example, all the ugliness involved in orthodox marriage, so you say, "I shall never get married," and you throw yourself into social work instead; or perhaps your parents have urged you into it, or you have an ideal. If it is a means of escape, or if you are merely pursuing an ideal established by society, by a leader or a priest, or by yourself, then any social work you may do will only create further misery. But if you have love in your heart, if you are seeking truth and are therefore a truly religious person, if you are no longer ambitious, no longer pursuing success, and your virtue is not leading to respectability—then your very life will help to bring about a total transformation of society.

I think it is very important to understand this. When we are young, as most of you are, we want to do something, and social work is in the air; books tell about it, the newspapers do propaganda for it, there are schools to train social workers, and so on. But you see, without self-knowledge, without understanding yourself and your relationships, any social work you do will turn to ashes in your mouth.

It is the happy man, not the idealist or the miserable escapee, who is revolutionary; and the happy man is not he who has many possessions. The happy man is the truly religious man, and his very living is social work. But if you become merely one of the innumerable social workers, your heart will be empty. You may give away your money, or persuade other people to contribute theirs, and you may bring about marvellous reforms; but as long as your heart is empty and your mind full of theories, your life will be dull, weary, without joy. So, first understand yourself, and out of that self-knowledge will come action of the right kind.

Questioner: Why is man so callous?

KRISHNAMURTI: That is fairly simple, is it not? When education limits itself to conveying knowledge and preparing the student for a job, when it merely holds up ideals and teaches him to be concerned with his own success, obviously man becomes callous. You see, most of us have no love in our hearts. We never look at the stars or delight in the whispering waters; we never observe the dance of moonlight on a rushing stream or watch the flight of a bird. We have no song in our hearts; we are always occupied; our minds are full of schemes and ideals to save mankind; we profess brotherhood, and our very look is a denial of it. That is why it is important to have the right kind of education while we are young, so that our minds and our hearts are open, sensitive, eager. But that eagerness, that energy, that explosive understanding is destroyed when we are afraid; and most of us are afraid. We are afraid of our parents, of our teachers, of the priest, of the government, of the boss; we are afraid of ourselves. So life becomes a thing of fear, of darkness, and that is why man is callous.

Questioner: Can one refrain from doing whatever one likes and still find the way to freedom?

KRISHNAMURTI: You know, it is one of the most difficult things to find out what we want to do, not only while we are adolescent, but throughout life. And unless you find out for yourself what you really want to do with your whole being, you will end by doing something which holds no vital interest for you, and then your life will be miserable; and, being miserable, you will seek distraction in cinemas, in drink, in reading innumerable books, in some kind of social reform and all the rest of it.

So, can the educator help you to find out what it is you want to do right through life, irrespective of what your parents and society may want you to do? That is the real question, is it not? Because, if once you discover what you love to do with your whole being, then you are a free man; then you have capacity, confidence, initiative. But if, without knowing what you really love to do, you become a lawyer, a politician, this or that, then there will be no happiness for you, because that very profession will become the means of destroying yourself and others.

You must find out for yourself what it is you love to do. Don't think in terms of choosing a vocation in order to fit into society, because in that way you will never discover what you love to do. When you love to do something, there is no problem of choice. When you love, and let love do what it will, there is right action, because love never seeks success, it is never caught up in imitation; but if you give your life to something which you don't love, you will never be free.

But merely doing whatever you like is not doing what you love to do. To find out what you really love to do requires a great deal of penetration, insight. Don't begin by thinking in terms of earning a livelihood; but if you discover what it is you love to do, then you will have a means of livelihood.

Questioner: Is it true that only the pure can be really fearless?

KRISHNAMURTI: Don't have ideals of purity, chastity, brotherhood, non-violence and all the rest of it, because they have no meaning. Don't *try* to be courageous, because that is merely a reaction to fear. To be fearless requires immense insight, an understanding of the whole process of fear and its cause.

You see, there is fear as long as you want to be secure—secure in your marriage, secure in your job, in your position, in your responsibility, secure in your ideas, in your beliefs, secure in your relationship to the world or in your relationship to God. The movement the mind seeks security or gratification in any form, at any level, there is bound to be fear; and what is important is to be aware of this process and understand it. It is not a matter of so-called purity. The mind which is alert, watchful, which is free of fear, is an innocent mind; and it is only the innocent mind that can understand reality, truth or God.

Unfortunately, in this country as elsewhere, ideals have assumed extraordinary importance, the ideal being the what *should* be: I should be non-violent, I should be good, and so on. The ideal, the what *should* be is always somewhere far away, and therefore it never *is*. Ideals are a curse because they prevent you from thinking directly, simply and truly, when you are faced with facts. The ideal, the what-*should*-be is an escape from what *is*. The what-*is* is the fact that you are afraid—afraid of what your parents will say, of what people will think, afraid of society, afraid of disease, death; and if you face what *is*, look at it, go into it even though it brings you misery, and understand it, then you will find that your mind becomes extraordinary simple, clear; and in that very clarity there is the cessation of fear. Unfortunately we are educated in all the philosophical absurdities of ideals, which are merely postponement; they have no validity at all.

You have the ideal of non-violence, for example; but are you non-violent? So why not face your violence, why not look at what you are? If you observe your own greed, your ambition, your pleasures and distractions, and begin to understand all that, you will find that time as a means of progress, as a means of achieving the ideal has come to an end. You see, the mind invents time in which to achieve, and therefore it is never quiet, never still. A still mind is innocent, fresh, though it may have had a thousand years of experience, and that is why it is able to resolve the difficulties of its own existence in relationship.

Questioner: Man is the victim of his own desires, which create many problems. How can he bring about a state of desirelessness?

KRISHNAMURTI: Wanting to bring about a state of desirelessness is merely a trick of the mind. Seeing that desire creates misery and wanting to escape from it, the mind projects the ideal of desirelessness and then asks, "How am I to achieve that ideal?" And then what happens? In order to be desireless you suppress your desire, do you not? You throttle your desire, you try to kill it, and then you think you have achieved a state of desirelessness—which is all false.

What is desire? It is energy, is it not? And the moment you throttle your energy you have made yourself dull, lifeless. That is what has happened in India. All the so-called religious men have throttled their desire; there are very few who think and are free. So, what is important is not to throttle desire, but to understand energy and the utilization of energy in the right direction.

You see, when you are young you have abounding energy—energy that makes you want to skip over the hills, reach for the stars. Then, society steps in and tells you to hold that energy within the walls of the prison which it calls respectability. Through education, through every form of sanction and control, that energy is gradually crushed out. But you need *more* energy, not less, because without immense energy you will never find out what is true. So the problem is not how to curtail energy, but how to maintain and increase it, how to make it independent and continuous—but not at the behest of any belief or society—so that it becomes the movement towards truth, God. Then energy has quite a different significance. As a pebble thrown into a calm lake creates an ever-widening circle, so the action of energy in the direction of what is true creates the waves of a new culture. Then, energy is limitles, immeasurable, and that energy is God.

Index to Questions